Modern Management Accounting Developments

Financial Times Management Briefings are happy to receive proposals from individuals who have expertise in the field of management education.

If you would like to discuss your ideas further, please contact Andrew Mould, Commissioning Editor.

Tel: 0171 447 2210
Fax: 0171 240 5771
e-mail: andrew.mould@pitmanpub.co.uk

FINANCIAL TIMES
Management Briefings

Finance

Modern Management Accounting Developments

FALCONER MITCHELL

CHRIS SALAFATINOS

FT
PITMAN
PUBLISHING

London • Hong Kong • Johannesburg • Melbourne • Singapore • Washington DC

PITMAN PUBLISHING
128 Long Acre, London WC2E 9AN
Tel: +44 (0)171 447 2000
Fax: +44 (0)171 240 5771

A Division of Pearson Professional Limited

First published in Great Britain 1997

ISBN 0 273 63238 8

British Library Cataloguing in Publication Data
A CIP catalogue record for this book can be obtained from the British Library.

10 9 8 7 6 5 4 3 2 1

Printed and bound in Great Britain

The Publishers' policy is to use paper manufactured from sustainable forests.

About the authors

Falconer Mitchell is professor of management accounting at the University of Edinburgh. He has researched and taught management accounting for over twenty years. His current interests include Japanese cost management, uniform costing, activity based costing and performance measurement.

Chris Salafatinos is lecturer in accounting at the University of Edinburgh. He was previously financial controller of a medium sized engineering company based in Chicago. In 1996 he completed his doctorate based on a grounded theory study of the implementation of activity based costing in a gas company.

CONTENTS

1 Introduction

The Nature of Management Accounting

The potential functions of the management accountant are many and varied (see Figure 1.1). In essence however, the management accountant is in the information business. His/her responsibilities ultimately lie in providing information to underpin the key managerial activities of organisational planning, decision-making, improving and controlling. Underlying the role of the management accountant is the economic motive which in a private sector context relates to profitability and in the not-for-profit sector to resource use and cost management. Consequently management accounting is concerned with the provision of information on the above managerial activities which ultimately relates to their financial impact. Thus in the private sector context, the development and expression of plans in terms of their profitability implications, the identification of the profit impact of the different options facing decision-makers and the production of attention directing reports on the various stages in profit earning lie at the core of good management accounting practice.

A	Provide management accounting services & systems
B	Manage management accounting staff
C	Assure the quality of services and systems
D	Plan and arrange finance
E	Utilise intelligence from outside sources
F	Provide planning services
G	Guide management decisions
H	Analyse, report and interpret the organisation's performance to management
I	Present reports and accounts for investors

Figure 1.1 Key Roles of the Management Accountant.

Source: Standards of Competence in Management Accountancy, Chartered Institute of Management Accountants, London, August, 1993.

Required Guidelines

The quality of the information service provided by the management accounting function depends upon both the relevance and reliability of the information provided to management. The former attribute is based upon ensuring the pertinence of information to the pursuit of the profit of the organisation's economic (usually profit) objective. To achieve information relevance the management accountant must appreciate managerial information needs. This requires close contact with the managerial function to gain familiarisation with the situations in which an accounting input would be appropriate and to act as analyst and interpreter particularly where the information is technically complex. Relevant proactivity by the management accountant is fostered by this type of close contact between accountant and manager. Reliability of information is dependent on the objectivity and technical efficacy of the management accounting practices in use. Much of the information produced by management accountants comprises future estimates. In making these, objectivity can only be retained by avoiding subjective influences (e.g. biasing in favour of sectional interests in the organisation) when making the estimate. In a complex social and political environment this may be difficult to achieve. Most management accounting practices also have technical limitations (e.g. in allocating costs to products) and the information which may be generated (often due to constraints of time and cost) is often not ideal. The management accountant therefore has a responsibility to identify these limitations for managerial users to ensure that they are sensitive to them when making use of accounting information. While current developments in management accounting may improve the technical aspects of information they do not usually eliminate all deficiencies nor do they negate the behavioural factors at play during the management accounting process. Care still has to be taken in using them and their limitations must be identified and communicated to users.

Structure of Text

This text is based on the review of a whole series of different types of management accounting information, emphasising recent developments in what has recently become a very dynamic area. Not only is the nature of these techniques presented but an assessment of their main strengths and weaknesses is provided. The text is structured round the main managerial activities which accounting information can support. Chapter 2 outlines different ways in which the management accountant can contribute to the establishment of organisational strategy. Chapter 3 focuses on the translation of strategic objectives into practical operational guidelines. Chapter 4 relates how performance can be measured to indicate progress towards the organisation's objectives. Chapters 5 and 6 are concerned with how performance can be improved with, respectively, the new activity based approaches to cost management and a range of innovative techniques centred on business processes and products. Chapter 7 specifically examines decision support information and finally some conclusions are drawn in Chapter 8.

2   Strategic management accounting

Management Accounting and Strategy

Corporate strategy is concerned with the establishment of organisational objectives and the devising of means by which these objectives can be attained. It thus involves the development of ways of coping effectively with a competitive environment over the medium to long term. Strategy is based on gaining competitive advantage either by pricing advantage (perhaps based on cost superiority) or by differentiating product or service output in a manner which makes them particularly attractive to potential customers. Management accounting information can support strategy development and operation in a number of ways:

- by providing accounting based analyses of the market context in which the firm will operate

- by providing key information linked to selected strategies, e.g. product cost information for those aiming to be low cost producers in order to assist management to succeed in their chosen course of action

- by providing feedback on the success or otherwise of recent performance in pursuit of particular strategies

- by providing information on the longer term implications of alternative courses of action.

This chapter examines some of the major techniques that have been suggested as appropriate for strategic level decision making. Together they have become known as strategic management accounting.

Value Chain Analysis

A value chain analysis ensures that the organisation is viewed in terms of its overall setting within the appropriate industrial sector and market environment. The value chain is thus an industry level concept and is concerned with enhancing all of the activities associated with the industry wide chain of events which convert raw materials into products or services for the end consumer. It is designed to highlight which activities generate profit and, from further analysis, to identify the key factors which drive costs at each point in the value chain. For example a simplified value chain for potato crisp production is shown in Figure 2.1 below.

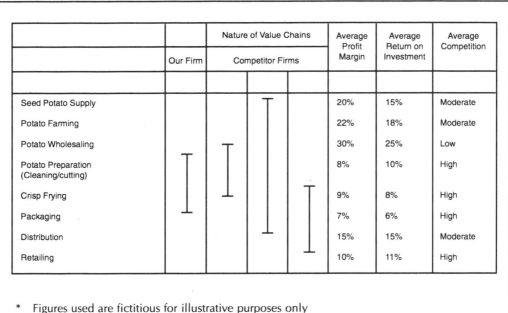

		Nature of Value Chains		Average Profit Margin	Average Return on Investment	Average Competition
	Our Firm	Competitor Firms				
Seed Potato Supply				20%	15%	Moderate
Potato Farming				22%	18%	Moderate
Potato Wholesaling				30%	25%	Low
Potato Preparation (Cleaning/cutting)				8%	10%	High
Crisp Frying				9%	8%	High
Packaging				7%	6%	High
Distribution				15%	15%	Moderate
Retailing				10%	11%	High

* Figures used are fictitious for illustrative purposes only

Figure 2.1 Potato crisp value chain.

This framework provides a comprehensive analysis of (a) where the costs of the total industrial process are incurred and (b) how the revenue ultimately derived from the end user is distributed across the value chain. In effect, the location of profit earning activities is highlighted. It allows a supra-firm analysis involving questions such as: which activity earns the greatest profit? Which activities are our competitors involved in? Where is competition most intensive? The analysis thus supports strategic analysis on integration policy and on the possibilities of negotiation with suppliers and customers on costs and prices.

Moreover this type of analysis facilitates comparisons with competitors who may often encompass different parts of the value chain. Differences in performance can initiate further internal analyses of how effectively activities are managed. For example, the important factors driving cost for each activity can be identified and performance assessed from this perspective. Michael Porter has suggested that differentiation between structural and executional cost drives can provide a suitable basis for this type of analysis (see Figure 2.2).

Structural Cost Drivers	Executional Cost Drivers
• Scale of operation • Scope (vertical integration) of operation • Experience of activity • Technology employed • Complexity of operation	• Quality • Capacity utilisation • Work force capability • Product design • Plant/process design • Supplier/customer relations

Figure 2.2 Cost driver analysis.

Different activities in the value chain may well be influenced by different cost drivers but within the total set exist the sources of potential improvement for the organisation. However costs must be balanced with revenues. Moreover initiatives to differentiate by providing enhanced value at any stage of the value chain may merit the investment of resource and extra cost.

In these ways value chain analysis provides a fundamental framework for the strategic assessment of the organisation's current position within the market sector and its potential for future development. Although often difficult to construct and requiring many estimates, the absence of this type of information may leave management in the dark as to how competitors are more successful and how a more competitive strategy can be developed.

Market Centred Information

Bringing the market into the firm through the management accounting system provides another opportunity to highlight strategic considerations. The following sections provide a review of four types of information which will internalise the market context of the organisation and promote managerial awareness of the need to consider action in the competitive environment which exists for their firm.

Product Grid Analysis

Final products and services can be categorised in terms of a variety of dimensions which indicate their strategic potential to the organisation. Their placing in respect of these characteristics can guide management in their assessment of the strategic potential of product lines to the organisation. Figure 2.3 demonstrates how products can be allocated to one of four quarters of a grid matching potential sales volume and profitability. The location of the product helps to determine (a) how it might contribute to policy and (b) how its financial performance might be improved.

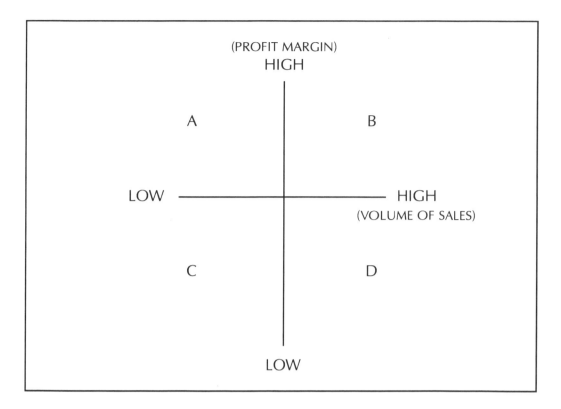

Figure 2.3 Product profitability.

The products falling into cell A may benefit from strategies which can increase their sales volume while maintaining margins (or possibly by reducing selling price and margin if elasticity of demand is great) while those in cell C are candidates for dropping as they offer little potential in either volume or profit terms. Products in cell B are 'stars' and merit strategies to foster their position while those falling in cell D require more effective cost control or higher selling prices to boost margins. Some variability in the type of axis used is possible with, for example, a contribution margin being used for the vertical measure for shorter term analysis and a full cost (perhaps based on the activity based costing approach – see Chapter 5) based margin for longer term analysis. The use of growth potential rather than historic volume may also enhance the strategic implications of the y axis.

Customer Profitability Analysis

Profit is realised only through commercial transactions with customers. It is natural therefore to consider the individual customer as a focus for profitability analysis and in this way to identify and locate profit in the facet of the market where it has been earned. This type of analysis can identify the customer relationships to be fostered, those which require redefinition (e.g. in pricing or distribution arrangements) and those where termination may be considered. Indeed the grid analysis of the preceeding section is again useful in this context with customers replacing products as the focus of analysis. In order to derive customer profitability analysis, production and non-production costs have to be traced to the customer with reasonable accuracy and again activity based costing systems (see Chapter 5) have been prominent in providing a means of doing this.

While individual customers can be assessed from this perspective an organisation can also obtain a view of its overall profitability through the construction of a cumulative distribution which will provide a more general indication of the success of its customer oriented strategies (see Figure 2.4). For example from Figure 2.4 it would be brought to the management's attention that 25% of customers are lossmaking and the potential exists to improve overall profitability from revising the trading relationship with them.

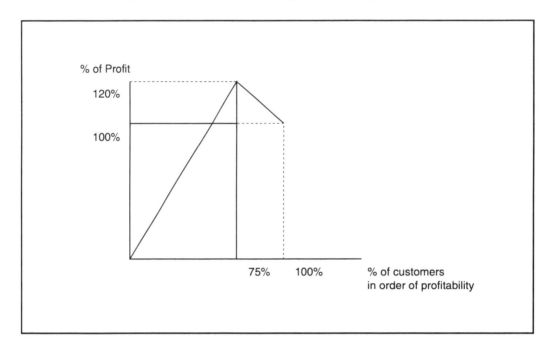

Figure 2.4

Competitor Analysis

Comparisons with leading competitors provide a rich source of ideas for improvement and strategic change as well as indications of the success of selected strategies. Perhaps the most common approach to this is through the operation of inter-firm comparison schemes. These are conveniently based on ratio analysis of the financial statements of the participating organisations and may extend to a level of detail only available from internal accounting reports. The specification of the selected ratios into sector averages and upper and lower quartiles can assist the user to place their company in the sectional league and identify where (as opposed to the detail of how) the best performers are gaining their advantage. This concept may also be extended in a more open way in benchmarking relationships normally with companies of comparable size in non-competing business areas. This is particularly useful for the assessment of central service resourcing and performance, e.g. administration, finance, purchasing, and even research and development. Finally some key intelligence may be gathered from close competitors through product cost comparisons particularly where competitive strategies are based on pricing or product design differentiation. This type of information normally has to be gathered without the co-operation of the competitor. However the competitors' products can be purchased and broken down by engineers to reveal the components used and give insights into the assembly process and product design. This information in conjunction with other data collected from company visits and observation, press reports, ex members of staff, prospectuses and annual reports can provide the basis for reasonable estimates of full product costs which can highlight comparative advantages and disadvantages for further exploration and assessment.

The Prevailing Market Conditions

Feedback on performance can be given a strategic orientation by internalising some of the market assessment undertaken when establishing policies and strategy. One way of achieving this is to incorporate market size and market share variances into the internal performance reports produced for management. This not only highlights the planning and forecasting ability of the organisation but also allows actual performance to be assessed in the light of prevailing market conditions. Strategy which may be predicated on market expectations can then be better reviewed. Figure 2.5 illustrates the computation of these variances.

The variances are computed by comparing the profit which would have been earned had the market size and share estimates been correct (column (1)) with the profit from holding the expected market share in the smaller than expected actual market (column (2)). The market shrinkage cost the organisation £1 million in lost profits. However not only was market size unfavourably small but market share was lost from the expected 5% down to an actual 3.3% (500,000 units ÷ 15 million units). This has eroded profits by a further £1 million. Thus the variances may signal the need for improved forcasting and/or a revision of strategy to deal with depressed market conditions and the loss of market share.

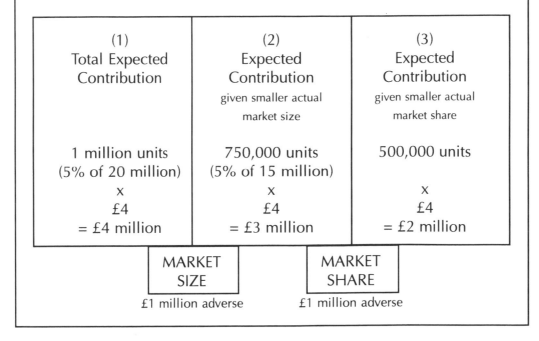

Organisational strategy and plans are based on the following estimates:

Total Market	–	20 million units
Market Share (our firm)	–	5% of total market
Expected Unit Contribution	–	Selling price £10
		Variable cost £ 6
		Contribution £ 4

The actual total market proved to be 15 million units and actual sales were 500,000 units.

VARIANCES:

(1) Total Expected Contribution	(2) Expected Contribution given smaller actual market size	(3) Expected Contribution given smaller actual market share
1 million units (5% of 20 million) x £4 = £4 million	750,000 units (5% of 15 million) x £4 = £3 million	500,000 units x £4 = £2 million

MARKET SIZE   MARKET SHARE

£1 million adverse   £1 million adverse

Figure 2.5 Market size and share variances.

Shareholder Value Analysis

Strategy can only be effective if it influences decision making at the highest level within the organisation. One framework for establishing this important link is shareholder value analysis. This approach assumes a rational, economic perspective for managerial strategy which is aimed at producing the highest (present) value for the organisation for its shareholders. Strategy should be set to enhance this value and strategic decisions determined by their impact on the financial value of the organisation. As future cash flows underlie economic value, strategy should be established to maximise their present value. Thus key drivers of future cash flows become the most important influences on strategic decisions. For example sales growth, profit margin, investment cost of capital and working capital management may be viewed as central to current value. These factors provide a basis upon which competing strategies can be assessed. The key question is which strategy produces the pattern of future cash flows that will, when discounted, give the highest net present value for the organisation? Strategies can also be developed to enhance sales growth, working capital management or indeed to reduce the cost of capital used to discount the future cash flows.

This approach can be complemented by focusing on present values and future cash flows as a basis for assessing the performance of the key divisions or segments of the organisation which operationalise strategy. For example divisional performance could be assessed on the basis of the division's net present value derived from discounting the management's estimate of future maintainable net cash inflows. If this measurement is repeated at regular intervals the divisional manager can be held accountable for delivering the cash flow estimate for the most recent period and justifying any movement in the divisional net present value. The feedback system thus matches the shareholder value analysis philosophy, is forward looking in orientation and employs the information which is most appropriate for the strategic decision making (i.e. cash flows).

Conclusion

Strategic management accounting is a relatively new development but it is one that offers scope for considerable innovation in management accounting. This is particularly so in applying to accounting some of the economic analyses which can be related to market behaviour. For example the measurement and quantitative assessment of barriers to entry for pricing policy, of the strength of suppliers and their ability to resist downward supply price pressure and of customer options and of the significance of price vis-à-vis other product attributes are all valid areas where the management accountant could develop strategy relevant information.

3   Guiding the organisation

Setting and Using Budgets

Budgets provide a mechanism for translating the strategy of the organisation into meaningful short and medium term performance expectations. While at one level these are expressed in financial terms in the form of periodic end results (financial statements), they also encompass the segmentation of aggregate results to areas of responsibility which provide operational guidance and control. The hierarchical nature of the budget and its decomposition into subareas of responsibility thus provides scope for building it from the bottom up or, alternatively, from the top down. In the former instance the budgeted financial statements are the end result of the process and in the latter they are the starting point. The first approach has the advantages of facilitating the participation of those involved at an operational level in setting the budget to which they are subject. This has several potential advantages and drawbacks. The resultant budget is more likely to be perceived as attainable and therefore represents a more realistic plan of action for the organisation. Its acceptance and ownership by those subject to it are more readily achieved and thus the motivation to attain it is greater. However, this approach also has its drawbacks. Top management have less influence on the type of standard set by the budget and its fit to the strategy and goals of the firm is thereby made more difficult. In addition the bottom up approach increases the opportunities for slack to be built into the budget as those held accountable for each area of responsibility attempt to ensure that the budget benchmark against which they will be judged is easily attainable. While budget imposition by top management may alleviate these problems it also fails to achieve the behavioural advantages of the participative approach. Consequently a compromise approach involving several iterative modifications may allow some of the beneficial aspects of both budgetary styles to be achieved. In this way the budget can contribute to both the planning and control functions of the organisation.

Technical Aspects

(a) The Setting Process

At a more technical level both the budget orientation and flexibility have to be considered. All budgets should reflect both the internal capabilities of the firm and the external opportunities which may be available to it. Each of these aspects is an important determinant of budget realism. However the starting point of the budgetary process determines which will provide the orientation of the budget. Thus budgetary plans may begin with the estimation of external sales or estimation of possible production levels. The former ensures that production plans are set to meet market demand and is therefore more likely to avoid over or under production (particularly in dynamic markets) with build ups or shortfalls of stock. This type of budget is tailored to meet the expected sales figure with each area of responsibility being set a target derived from the sales goal. The process is outlined vertically in Figure 3.1.

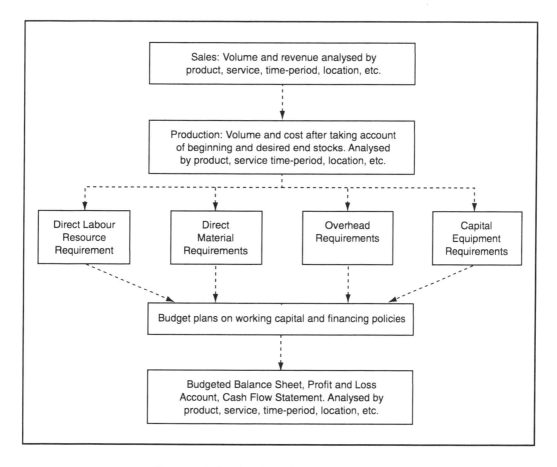

Figure 3.1 The budgetary process.

(b) Budget Flexibility and Revision

The budgetary process outlined in Figure 3.1 is initially conducted before the start of the period to which it pertains. It is therefore based on the expected conditions in the product or service market and the factor markets in which the firm operates. If these change significantly then the budget loses much of its value both as a plan and a standard for comparison. To overcome this problem the original (or fixed) budget can be subject to a process of revision. For example an annual budget may be revised quarterly to reflect how actual performance has matched up to initial expectations and to adjust for better informed estimates of the remaining portion of the year. In this way the budget retains its credibility and its power to motivate.

While revisions can be achieved by complete reviews of the budget components, an important element of revision can also be systematically built into the budgetary process. This involves operating on the basis of flexible budgeting and standard costing. This approach is widely adopted in the UK and USA manufacturing sectors, although it is also applicable to many service sector situations. Essentially it involves the estimation of the expected or budget costs (standard cost) and revenues (standard price) for one unit of output. These are then used to 'flex' the financial budget to reflect the actual levels of production and sales volumes achieved in sales and production in the period. Flexing simply involves multiplying the actual volumes achieved in sales and production by the standard costs and prices to produce a budget revision which not only reflects the actual activity levels attained but which also still attributes expected costs and revenues to them. The use of standard costs allows detailed information to be computed on how actual and flexed budget performance have differed. This is known as cost variance analysis. The cost variances are segmented to reflect how much of the variance has been caused by the actual acquisition cost of the resource differing from standard and how much is due to the difference (between actual and standard) in the efficiency (as compared with standard) with which the acquired resource has been used. For example Figure 3.2 illustrates how the direct material cost variance is segmented (similar segmentation can be carried out for sales and the other cost elements) and linked to areas of managerial responsibility. The price variance is the responsibility of the purchasing manager and the usage variance the responsibility of the production manager.

The final product has a standard allowance of 2 kilos of direct material which should be purchased for £1 per kilo. Actually 1000 units of the final product were produced and this involved the use of 2200 kilos at a total cost of £2,500.

(1) Actual Cost of Production 1000 units
     using 2200 kilos cost   = £2,500

                                                                   Price Variance £300
                                                                   unfavourable

(2) Actual Cost of Material at standard price
     2200 kilos @ £1   = £2,200

                                                                   Usage Variance £200
                                                                   unfavourable

(3) Total Standard Cost of 1000 units produced = £2,000

Figure 3.2 Direct material standard cost variance.

Standard costing can thus provide a considerable enhancement to cost control and to performance assessment. However, in its conventional form it does suffer from certain disadvantages. Firstly, it can be problematic and costly to operate in situations where products are complex and subject to regular adaptation and change. For example the large volume of parts in a PC and the regular alterations made to their design would make the maintenance of a relevant standard cost a difficult task. Second the flexing of the budget is really appropriate only for the variable elements of cost (materials, labour and some overheads which vary with the volume of final output). Finally the significance of factors such as efficiency which can affect the volume of final output are measured only in terms of cost difference from standard. Their full economic effect on profitability (for example, through producing more or less than expected) is not reported. The latter drawback can be coped with by using the standard contribution margin (standard selling price less standard variable cost – see Chapter 7 for further discussion of the contribution margin) multiplied by the volume difference (for example the extra units produced and sold as a result of abnormally high efficiency) as a measure of profit gained or foregone by each factor influencing the volume of output.

(c) Planning and Operational Variances

Finally the idea of using a budget or standard cost benchmark as a means for assessing performance may be further extended by considering a revision of the standard and budget immediately after the end of the period under review. This ensures that the standard cost components and the budget volume are determined with the benefit of hindsight and therefore come closer to reflecting the best possible performance attainable in the period. Not only is a rigorous basis for judging actual performance obtained but a method of separating budget variances into the amounts caused by poor estimates when setting the budget (planning variance) and those caused by abnormally poor or good operational performance (operational variance) is created. Figure 3.3 shows the basis for this type of analysis.

Comparison of the 'budgets' produced at the beginning and end of the period produces the planning variance while the comparison of the 'ex post' budget with actual performance is attributable to operational causes.

Zero, Priority and Activity-Based Budgets

(a) The Basic Approach

While costs such as direct materials and direct labour are primarily determined by the volume of final output there are many other costs whose proper levels are much less easy to decide. Support services such as maintenance, scheduling, logistics, set-up, quality control, purchasing, customer order liaison and administration are all important areas of resource consumption whose costs may not have a readily apparent relationship with pure output volume. For them the setting, review and revision of the budget can therefore benefit from the adoption of zero and/or activity based approaches.

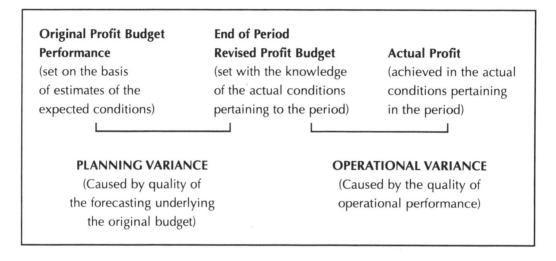

Figure 3.3 Planning and operational variances.

The activity based approach to budgeting involves identifying the activities and sub-activities which make up the support services of the organisation. For example customer liaison activity may comprise

•   Credit control vetting of customers

•   Order receipt and processing

•   Despatch of orders

•   Customer enquiries and returns

•   Debt collection

•   Maintenance of sales records.

This type of profiling, which also attributes cost to each activity, gives visibility to the way in which resources are consumed in customer order liaison and this can provide a starting point for (a) assessing resource needs in the area and (b) deciding on the value of each dimension of the service for the organisation. For example debt collection might be expanded or reduced in size, handled in house or subcontracted to an external agency. Moreover the fee quotation from an agency would provide a useful comparator for the budget requests from the existing internal unit. Any non-value added (activities which do not generate value for the end customer) aspects of the service may also come to light in this type of analysis and so provide an immediate basis for targeting budget cuts.

(b) Cost Drivers

The availability of cost driver volumes can also assist both the budget setting process and the provision of cost variance feedback information. Cost drivers are measures indicative of the level of work throughput in each activity. Examples would include the number of new customers (customer vetting), the number of orders received (order processing and despatch), the number of customer returns (customer enquiries and return), the number of debts over 2 months old (debt collection). Cost driver estimates provide a basis for identifying the future resource needs for each of the activities. Projected increases in cost driver volumes can provide a legitimate case for increasing a particular budget. In effect, with an activity based approach, resource needs have a quantifiable foundation which can guide resource allocation. Moreover when a budget is set then an expected cost for each work activity can be established from cost driver projections (e.g. number of orders to be processed, number of customer returns etc.) by applying the 'standard' cost of each unit of activity (and allowing for any 'fixed' element of cost). At the very least those involved in budget setting can see whether more or less work is to be undertaken and so judge and negotiate on resource bids with this knowledge.

Feedback on budget/actual performance comparisons are also enhanced by the use of an activity framework for the budgetary process. Not only is each activity given visibility but through the availability of projected and actual cost driver information capacity usage and spending variances can be produced. Management can therefore quickly identify where there are consistent over/under provisions of capacity and where control over spending is weak or strong (see Figure 3.4 for illustration). In essence budget variance relevance is enhanced by using a range of work volume measures in addition to simply the final output volume to flex the budget.

(c) Zero Basis

The activity based approach to budgeting also provides a solid foundation for the operation of zero based budgeting. This requires budget holders to begin from scratch and provide a rationale for all resources requested as opposed to simply building a case on the basis of an increment to the previous year's budget. It is a mechanism which can counter empire building and organisational slack as all resource use is scrutinised, but it can be time consuming and can appear threatening to staff particularly where they consider their employment to be at risk. Consequently it is not normally used as a routine approach to budget setting but one which may be used occasionally, perhaps every five or so years as a means of halting the proliferation of cost. The activity and sub-activity analyses outlined above provide a convenient means of detailing the nature and justification for resource requests from the zero base at budget time. Each sub-activity can be ranked or prioritised in terms of its importance to service provision and the implications of funding removal or reduction for it can be clearly identified. This provides central management with some guidance for determining the level of funding provided to each area of the business and also which sub-activities to fund where choices have to be made. In prioritising budget funding the alternative volumes and qualities of service should be known and inform the resource allocation changes. Figure 3.5 summarises the information which can profile the service level possibilities for ordering and which can be of particular assistance in building the budget from a zero base.

Budgeted Cost per   =   Budgeted Purchasing Cost   =   £500,000   =   £5 per order
Purchase Order   Volume of Purchase Order   100,000 orders

                        Capacity provided

Assuming the budgeted volume of purchase orders for the period to be 96,000 (ie. 5000 less than the capacity provided) the actual volume of purchase order as 90,000 and the actual spend as £400,000 the variance analysis is as follows:

(1)   Charged to products 90,000* x £5 =   450,000
(2)   Planned unused capacity 4,000** x £5 =   20,000   Unfavourable
(3)   Capacity utilisation 6000*** x £5 =   30,000   Unfavourable
(4)   Spending Variance (£500,000 - £400,000)   100,000   Favourable

      ACTUAL COST OF PURCHASING   400,000

*   Actual volume
**   Capacity provided less budget volume
***   Budget volume less actual volume

Figure 3.4 Activity based budget feedback.

Activity Title: Supply Procurement Possible Budget Resource Provision	Level 1 Basic Provision £300,000	Level 2 Basic Provision £375,000	Level 3 Basic Provision £500,000
Resultant Service Implications: Capacity Provided	50,000 orders	60,000 orders	80,000 orders
Lead time for order execution	2 days	1.5 days	1 day
Expected error levels in orders	5%	3%	1%
New supplier vetting	Basic		Extended

Figure 3.5 Activity information for zero based budgeting.

Kaizen and Target Costing

(a) Kaizen Costing

The concept of Kaizen or continuous improvement is solidly entrenched in the operational practice of leading Japanese companies. While this approach encompasses virtually all aspects of activity and includes the suggestions of all employees for improving the methods of working it has also been explicitly linked to management accounting through Kaizen costing. This, as the name suggests, simply means the continuous improvement (or reduction) of cost. Thus cost measurement becomes an important component of the improvement system. The cost object for this purpose can vary but will relate to areas over which individuals have some influence (e.g. department, support service, final product or service output). Instead of budget targets being established in these areas the previous period's actual result becomes the target to be attained. This fits the philosophy of continuous improvement as the Kaizen costing system promotes a regular cost reduction over time trend. Improvement means beating last quarter's, month's or week's cost. The target is set by regular measurement of cost. This approach can be applied throughout the organisation using appropriate cost objects for each level in the hierarchy from factory floor to divisional manager. The pressure to meet the strategic demands of low cost production are thus translated, in a meaningful way, to all employees.

(b) Target Costing

However with the Japanese company the control and reduction of cost is, typically, also subject to the competitive demands of the market place. This is achieved by the widespread operation of systems of target costing where the cost levels to be attained are derived from market analysis. Figure 3.6 identifies the high level of popularity and some of the variety of this approach throughout many of the key industrial sectors in Japan. Target costing is product centred and involves the achievement of a market derived cost plan to drive and guide the planning, development, design and production of products. This involves the identification and satisfaction of market needs on price and other product attributes. The producer, often in conjunction with their suppliers, aims to supply a product which will meet customer needs for functionality and price and which will also deliver an acceptable level of profitability. As outlined in Figure 3.7, to translate these broad objectives into significant goals for employees a target cost is first derived from analysis of the expected market situation.

n		Pattern of Response	Used	Firmwide Application	Some Divisions	Some Projects	Not Used
26	14.4	Transportation Equipment	14.4	9.4	2.8	2.2	0
33	18.3	Machinery/Equipment	15.0	9.4	5.0	0.6	3.3
26	14.4	Electrical	12.8	8.9	1.7	2.2	1.6
28	15.6	Metals	6.1	2.2	2.8	1.1	9.5
11	6.1	Oil Rubber Glass	2.2	1.7	0.5	0	3.9
32	17.7	Chemical	5.6	1.2	2.2	2.2	12.2
6	3.3	Textiles	2.2	0	1.7	0.5	1.1
7	3.9	Food	1.1	0	0.5	0.6	2.8
5	2.8	Paper and Pulp	0	0	0	0	2.8
6	3.4	Other	1.1	0	1.1	0	2.3
180	100.0		60.5	32.8	18.3	9.4	39.5

Figure 3.6 Adoption of target costing in Japan.

Source: Tani T., et al, "Target Cost Management in Japanese Companies: Current State of the Art," Management Accounting Research, Vol. 5, 1994, pp. 67-81.

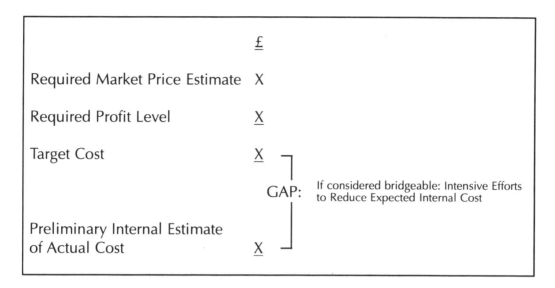

Figure 3.7 The target costing process.

This is translated into a cost level which can support the price. Then internal capabilities are assessed and likely costings undertaken. If the gap between the target cost and the internally derived cost estimates is considered bridgeable then the product development is considered viable but if not then plans are scrapped. Thus three stages are apparent in the target costing process: first the establishment of an expected market price; second the determination of the expected profit which allows this price to be translated into a target cost; third the elimination of the gap between target and expected actual cost. These we consider in turn below.

The foundation of target costing lies in the market research which underlies the determination of the price which customers will be prepared to pay for the final product. This is a task for those involved in marketing as it is based on the analysis of customer needs, potential product novelty, product differentiation and functionality and the prices of competing products.

From the set target price a deduction is made for the target profit. The residual is the target cost. The amount of this reduction depends upon the planned return on investment and profit margin for the organisation combined with the expected level of financial contribution required from the particular product under consideration. Normally at this stage a broad life cycle perspective will be taken to identify and ensure acceptability of projected margins and returns over the product's life.

Finally intensive efforts are made to close any gap between actual (or expected) and target cost. The primary thrust of this activity occurs before production plans are set i.e. at a stage where the decision committing the firm to costs has still to be made. This is one of the great strengths of the Japanese cost management system and one which differentiates it from Western approaches. A number of methods are used to push costs down. Suppliers are involved as 'partners' in the efforts to meet the target. This will involve targets being established for bought in parts and components and both supplier and producer will co-operate in their attainment. Designs will be modified to ensure high volume usage of key parts (perhaps through their incorporation in all models in the range) to ensure the benefits of economies of scale are enjoyed. The typical Japanese company will maintain cost tables which contain extensive up-to-date information on purchase prices of materials and the production costs of components using the latest technology. This information will be used in negotiations with suppliers to prompt them to keep prices down.

Internally the producer also makes continuous effort to contain costs. Underlying these efforts is the detailed information which is regularly produced on how resources are consumed within the firm. For example, Kousuu (see Figure 3.8) are produced for all aspects of the conversion costs of production. They are time based reports of how working hours have been spent. They contain the details of how resources have been consumed and explicitly target non value added aspects of work activity as cost reduction opportunities. The non-financial nature of Kousuu (they are expressed as time measurements) supports the Kaizen aproach at all levels in the hierarchy, facilitates the incorporation of employee suggestions for improvement and helps to maintain the momentum of cost reduction from pre-production through to the post-production stages of the product life cycle.

Finally the challenge of achieving the target cost is spread over many of the key personnel involved in new product development. This occurs partly by using multi-disciplinary teams to conduct value analysis and functional cost analysis (see Chapter 6 for details) on the whole product concept. These teams work under considerable pressure to deliver design suggestions and innovations which improve cost effectiveness. To facilitate their work, the cost target is frequently segmented into manageable sub-parts. This is frequently done on the basis of component product parts but product functions and departmental responsibilities provide other common bases for this segmentation. The product analysis is accompanied by obtaining customer views on the importance of product sub-functions and comparing the relative cost of these to their relative importance to the customer. This comparison signals where the match between resource consumption and customer value is not well aligned and so provides guidance on cost reduction efforts. Figure 3.9 illustrates the three step process which allows the target cost to become reality.

Type of working hours			
Working hours (WH)	Basic working hours	Net working hours (NWH)	1. machine loading and unloading 2. working manually or operating machines 3. supplying parts daily 4. washing processed parts and finished products 5. measuring processed parts and finished products
		Support activity working hours	1. walking between process 2. dressing parts and products 3. loading parts on automatic machines 4. adjusting machine tolerance 5. checking size of processed parts and finished products by random sampling 6. cleaning machinery
	Line management hours	Production peripheral working hours	1. turn on and off the main switches 2. preparing parts for manufacturing 3. preparing and checking tools 4. checking machine and supplying oil 5. cleaning machines and floors 6. warming up machines and training operators 7. holding preliminary meeting and making contact with workers 8. checking blueprint
		Incidental working hours	1. changing cutting or grinding oil 2. changing running or lubricating oil
		Set up hours	1. changing fitting and fixing tools 2. changing manufacturing tools
		Artificial delay hours	1. relating to abnormal shop floor works 2. relating to factory management 3. relating to personal issues
		Waiting hours	1. waiting for manufacturing parts and products

Figure 3.8 Working hours for Kousuu.

Source: Yoshikawa, T., 'Some Aspects of the Japanese Approach to Cost Management', Management Accounting Research, Vol.5, 1994, pp.279-287.

Stage 1   A matrix is constructed outlining (1) the importance of each product function from the customer's perspective and (2) the importance of each component part for each of the product functions (this is internally assessed). Where the value index differs significantly from 1.00 the component is targeted for possible cost reduction (under 1.00) or possible upgrading and investment (over 1).

Function	F1	F2	F3	F4	
Importance to customer	.3	.15	.5	.05	1.00
Component part:-					
C1	.6	.2	.5	.4	-
C2	.1	-	.4	.4	-
C3	.2	-	.1	-	-
C4	.1	.8	-	.2	-
	1.00	1.00	1.00	1.00	-

Stage 2   To identify the relative importance of each component in satisfying the customer's needs (final right hand column) a matrix is produced showing the results of multiplying the relative measures of importance of the functions by the contributions the components make to each function.

Function	F1	F2	F3	F4	
Importance to Customer	0.3	0.15	0.5	0.05	1.00
Component part:-					
C1	.18	.03	.25	.02	0.48
C2	.03	-	.2	.02	0.25
C3	.06	-	.05	-	0.11
C4	.03	.12	-	.01	0.16
	-	-	-	-	1.00

Stage 3   Compare the relative importance (reflecting the customer's perspective) of each component (as computed in stage 2) with their relative cost and compute a value index (former ÷ latter).

	Relative Importance	Relative Cost	Value Index
C1	.48	.30	1.600
C2	.25	.40	0.625
C3	.11	.10	1.1
C4	.16	.20	0.8

Where the Value Index is less than 1 the component is a target for cost reduction.

Figure 3.9 Functional analysis process.

4   Feedback on performance

Performance

Information on actual performance is necessary for a variety of important reasons. It provides feedback on the extent to which strategies are being successfully implemented and plans and budgets achieved. In addition, if its design permits, it facilitates assessment and analysis which can direct management to areas of strength which may be further exploited and areas of weakness where corrective action is merited. Thus performance reports should support constructive managerial action and for this purpose they require not only an appropriate content but also timely preparation.

Organisational performance is complex. It is multi-dimensional and therefore difficult to represent in the summary form required for manageable reports. There are also many technical problems associated with its translation into financial terms by the management accountant. Therein lies the challenge for the accountant of ensuring reliability and relevance. This chapter reviews performance measurement by examining the nature of and the problems associated with the more traditional financial based approach and exploring how these measures might be supplemented to overcome their disadvantages.

Financial Performance Measures

As budgets are normally set in financial terms and consolidated into conventional financial statement form (balance sheet, profit and loss account, cash flow statement) there is a strong tradition in management accounting of producing actual performance reports in similar form and devising key measures from the information which they contain. Moreover there has been considerable attraction for managers in distilling the contents of financial statements into one key general measure which indicates the overall level of performance achieved. This has the additional attraction of aligning internal systems with the type of information reported externally on corporate performance. Two accounting based measures have proved particularly popular and enduring.

(a) Return on Investment (and related ratios)

This ratio provides an overall indication of the end result performance of the organisation or a suitable segment of it. The numerator (see Figure 4.1) is a measure of the profit earned for the period under review and the denominator a measure of the investment which earned that profit. Depending upon the selection of the components the return measure can encompass different aspects of performance. For example it can reflect some or all of the manufacturing, trading, asset investment and financing elements of performance. Thus as a single measure, its great strength lies in the comprehensiveness of its coverage. Moreover it can be decomposed into contributory elements which allow more specific examination of how the return was made. For example, the incorporation of the sales figure allows the return to be split into two multiplicants (see Figure 4.2) which show how the intensity of asset use in generating sales and the average margin earned on sales combine to produce the ROI. This allows the analyst to assess how different divisional segments or products have achieved a particular ROI. The first sub-ratio measures asset productivity. Its use can turn managerial attention to the existence of under used or idle assets. The profit margin ratio reflects pricing policies adopted and the ability to control cost levels. Thus a high asset productivity low margin operation may earn a similar ROI to one with a lower productivity but higher margin. The use of the subsidiary ratio in conjunction with the ROI gives visibility to these differences and provides a basis for identifying the sources and causes of ROI variations. Despite its attractions as a performance measure, ROI suffers from two fundamental problems. First, because it is a ratio it discounts the effects of size. Thus an investment of £1,000 which earns the organisation £100 is viewed as equally beneficial to one of £1,000 million which earns £100 million. To illustrate further, Division A and Division B (see Figure 4.3) both have a current position ROI of 25%. The measure suggests no difference in performance. But if we consider their position on an incremental basis then Division B has achieved twice that of Division A. Division B offers everything Division A has achieved twice over. The achievements of successfully managing the larger scale operation and the much greater scale of the absolute amount of wealth generated by it are not reflected in the ROI indicator. The second problem of ROI is that the motivational impact of the measure may be dysfunctional to the organisation. Figure 4.3 (part II) illustrates how this may happen. Potential investment opportunities earning less than the current ROI will be unattractive as their acceptance results in an ROI reduction (see new position column).

$\dfrac{\text{Profit before interest}}{\text{Asset investment*}}$	x 100	Designed to reflect operational performance in trading and asset investment
$\dfrac{\text{Profit after interest and taxation}}{\text{Net asset investment**}}$	x 100	Designed to reflect operational performance and financial structure and tax management

*   This may represent total assets or if the full management of working capital were to be reflected then the deduction of current liabilities would be included

**   This would incorporate the deduction of long-term liabilities and given also the incorporation of interest and tax in the profit computation the ROI would reflect the effects of gearing and tax management

Figure 4.1 Return on investment measures.

$100 \times \dfrac{\text{Sales}}{\text{Asset investment}}$	x	$\dfrac{\text{Profit before tax and interest}}{\text{Sales}} \quad \text{x } 100$
A measure of the relative amount of sales generated from the assets available for use in the period		A measure of the profit margin earned on sales

Figure 4.2 The components of return on investment.

Similarly managers will be motivated to divest any separate parts of their business which earn less than the current ROI. While these actions do undoubtedly increase ROI they will not necessarily be in the interest of the business's owners. If the organisation's cost of capital is less than the ROI of any potential investments or divestments then despite the favourable ROI change the decision to increase or reduce the size of the operation will reduce the organisation's value. Any investment generating more than its cost of capital creates value. The use of ROI can therefore motivate managers to make decisions which reduce economic value but make their own performance appear better.

I DIVISIONAL COMPARISONS			
	DIVISION A	DIVISION B	DIFFERENCE
Profit	£1000	£2000	+ £1000
Investment	£4000	£8000	+ £4000
ROI	25%	25%	25%

II MOTIVATIONAL IMPACT OF ROI ON DECISIONS			
Effect of ROI on new investment decisions	Current Position	Potential Investment	New Position
Profit	£1000	£200	£1200
Investment	£4000	£1000	£5000
ROI	25%	20%	24% (reduced ROI)
Effect of ROI on divestment decisions	Current Position	Potential Investment	New Position
Profit	£2500	£700	£1800
Investment	£10000	£3000	£7000
ROI	25%	23.3%	25.7% (Increased ROI)

Figure 4.3 ROI – Dysfunctional consequences.

(b) Residual Income

General Electric, the USA utility, responded to the problems of ROI by developing their own performance measure, residual income, which has since become more widely used. This is also a profit based measure of performance which links the profit and loss account and balance sheet. However it does not suffer from the two ROI disadvantages outlined above and for this reason has become, particularly in the USA, widely used as a key measure of business and business segment performance.

Figure 4.4 illustrates both its computation and its effect on managerial behaviour. Residual income required one additional piece of information to that needed for ROI i.e. the organisation's cost of capital. Knowledge of this enables the relative size of business segments to be discounted by applying it to the investment base (which represents the capital invested). Thus a comparison of the current position of the two Divisions now reveals a relative performance which favours Division B (residual income £1,200 vs £600) as it has generated a greater absolute amount of wealth for its owners. Moreover the potential investment increases residual income while the divestment reduces it. The performance measure is therefore consistent with the proposition that decisions to increase size should be taken only where the extra investment more than covers the cost of capital and those relating to reductions in size only if the cost of capital avoided is greater than the trading profit which would be forgone.

Case 1 - Division A, Investment Opportunity	Current Position	Potential Investment	New Position
(1) Trading Profit	£1000	£200	£1200
(2) Investment	£4000	£1000	£5000
(3) Cost of Capital (10%) (2)	£400	£100	£500
(4) Residual Income (1) - (3)	£600	£100	£700
Case 2 - Division B, Divestment Opportunity	Current Position	Potential Investment	New Position
(1) Trading Profit	£2000	£200	£1800
(2) Investment	£8000	£1000	£7000
(3) Cost of Capital (10%) X (2)	£800	£100	£700
(4) Residual Income (1) - (3)	£1200	£100	£1100

Figure 4.4 Residual income.

While residual income overcomes two of the major ROI deficiencies it requires that the cost of capital is available. This is readily determined for loan capital which carries an explicit charge but is more problematic for equity (shareholders' funds). Conceptually equity is most appropriately represented as an opportunity cost, i.e. the cost of equity capital should represent the best alternative investment opportunities available to the owners. This is difficult to quantify and in practice surrogate measures have to be used. For example the earnings yield plus an expected annual growth percentage can provide a hurdle for new investments which ensures that current market expectations are impounded. However the expected growth element remains a subjective component of the capital cost figure.

Problems with Accounting-based Performance Measures

Four important limitations affect the value of the above approaches to organisational performance measurement. These problems are serious enough to cast doubt on the reliability of single financial performance indicators and they underlie the current trend towards producing packages of measures which permit the financial results to be viewed and assessed in context. The four major difficulties associated with ROI and residual income are as follows.

(a) Inflation

Inflation reduces both the general and the specific purchasing power of money, the measurement basis upon which financial performance indicators are computed. The former type of inflation renders a currency, say pounds, of different time periods different in terms of their general purchasing power. Thus a 1980 pound is different from a 1996 pound in a way similar to the difference between a franc and a dollar. This makes it difficult to sanction the conventional historic cost basis of accounting where, for example, the subtraction of pounds of cost at one point in time (e.g. a depreciation charge based on a historic acquisition cost) from pounds of revenue at a different point in time (current year sales) is a necessary step in computing a profit figure. Likewise the addition of different asset costs for the ROI denominator and as the basis for computing the cost of capital charge is questionable.

The latter type of inflation alters the financial implications of replacing resources which are consumed in business operations. For example if profit is only recognised after providing for specific inflation by charging against revenue the replacement cost of items sold then conventional historic cost approach. Moreover the return on investment and cost of capital charge may be based on the replacement cost of assets invested in the business in order to more realistically represent the current value of the investment made to earn the profit. Once again in times of inflation the specific conventional historic cost basis of asset valuation will result in ROI and residual income being overstated.

(b) Flexibility

Many of the procedures adopted by accountants in the preparation of financial statements offer scope for flexibility i.e. there are alternative treatments available which result in different financial results as reflected in the accounting performance measures produced. This problem affects the comparability of these measures between segments and over time. For example the decisions to write off development expenditure against profits or treat it as a fixed asset, to revalue land and buildings, to charge overheads to output, the method chosen to depreciate fixed assets and the estimation of their useful lives over which the write-offs take place all give scope for variation. The range of possible profit and asset investment figures can soon rise to large numbers as each area of choice combines multiplicatively (see below) to produce the possible number of end results.

Area of Choice	Development Expenditure		Depreciation Method		Overhead Rate Base		Fixed Asset Revaluation		
Number of Possibilities	2	X	4	X	4	X	2	=	64 different profits and asset values

(c) Short-Termism

In the short-term accounting performance measurements such as ROI and residual income can be manipulated by management to enhance reported profit. While this may be achieved by the choice of accounting procedures used (see previous section) it can also be done by taking operational decisions which increase profits, ROI and residual income over the following period but which can seriously reduce financial returns after that time. Examples include:

- Delaying the replacement of old equipment beyond the most appropriate date to avoid higher depreciation charges and asset investment figures.

- Deciding to reduce discretionary expenditure on training, advertising and research and development. The immediate effect is to reduce the costs charged against revenue in computing profit. The longer term effects however are adverse on profits through reduction of quality in staff inputs, loss of custom and lack of product innovation.

- The production of output for stock in excessive amounts. The inclusion of a proportion of fixed costs in the asset value of stock avoids charging them to profits and so this policy is profit enhancing until sales begin to exceed production.

- Window dressing working capital by paying off current liabilities earlier than necessary. This would reduce the asset investment figure where a total asset basis is used as a basis for its computation.

All of these actions have a real economic effect on the organisation i.e. they alter cash flows. In each case the overall effect is negative, sometimes extremely so, but they do allow the current and short-term reported accounting performance measures to look better.

(d) Timeliness

ROI and residual income are end-result measures. They are available only after the end of the period for which performance has been measured. While this means the measures can play a useful role in informing future operations and in guiding corrective action they do so only on a long lead time. They do not therefore facilitate timely preventative action. For this to occur some performance measures also need to precede the end results (see Figure 4.5). If the end result measures can be supplemented by measurements from the process and input stages then some forewarning of likely end results can be given and the feedback value of the performance measures enhanced. Indeed if the performance measurement system can be designed to precede even the input stage (e.g. by monitoring changes in supplier results and in the labour and equipment markets) then this aspect may be improved even further.

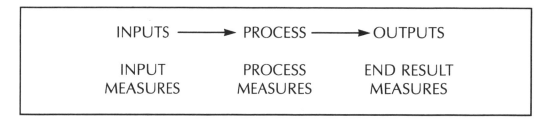

Figure 4.5 Performance measurement – stages.

Non-financial Performance Measures

Some of the problems associated with financial output measures can be alleviated by using non-financial supplements, for example measures of the physical volume of production and/or sales and of the volume of output returned by customers as unsatisfactory as opposed to their monetary representations. However, it is at the earlier stages of input and process that non-financial measures come into their own as feedback to instruct management action. Various aspects of process activity can be measured and these provide interim indications of aspects of performance which will ultimately impinge on the end results, for example the quantity and location of internal defects and waste, the amount of idle time and spare capacity, the existence of constraints and bottlenecks, the rate of consumption of energy, the nature of learning effects, the lead time and set up time for various work elements. All of these aid the monitoring process and can help pinpoint where and when action might be taken to mitigate the effect of problems on outputs. In addition non-financial measures of inputs can assist and indeed enhance the early warnings given by the performance measurement system. For example the age structure, volume, qualifications and experience of the labour force are all indicators which reflect factors with potential to eventually influence outcomes.

Finally non-financial measures can also provide a basis for providing information on the 'goodwill' resources of the firm which are normally omitted from financial reports. The skill, morale and motivation of the workforce underlie the human assets of the organisation and can all be measured non-financially. Likewise the location of the firm, the establishment of links with reliable sources of supply, the development of good long-term relationships with customers and the capacity to innovate and achieve flexibility in production are all attributes which impact on final outputs. Their individual state and changes therein are not however readily identifiable through conventional financial measurement. Non financial measures such as the results of employee attitude surveys, customer satisfaction surveys, and innovation rates (e.g. product life cycle lengths and rates of new product launches) can compensate for this deficiency. Their inclusion can thus help to identify policies which boost end results in the short-term but only at the expense of consuming goodwill and damaging longer term performances.

Non-financial measures can therefore focus on a whole variety of aspects of business performance. An extensive list of such measures, including those cited above, can readily be produced. However to be of most use some framework or structure has to be imposed on their selection and presentation and integration with financial measures. Two of the most topical structures for producing coherent batches of performance measures are outlined below.

The Critical Success Factor Approach

This approach is specifically designed to identify the key measures which relate to the achievement of objectives for an area of responsibility, business segment or indeed complete business entity. The process of performance measure selection commences with the identification of clear goals which are normally related to the otuputs or end-results of the focus for the exercise. For example, business goals may be set in terms of earnings per share or market share while those of a functional department might relate to the provision of a service on time and in the requisite quantity. Having specified objectives, analytical interviews are conducted with those involved in the work process to tease out where 'things must go right' in order for the goals to be attained. This analysis results in the critical success factors upon which performance is dependent. Consequently the performance measurement set is tailored to the particular situation under consideration. Its application will therefore result in different measures where circumsances differ. For example, the nature of the industry, of the competitive environment and of resource availability will all influence the CSF selection. Moreover as these contextual factors change over time so the CSFs require modification to maintain their suitability.

Underlying this approach is the application of user relevance to the measurement system. Ths CSFs provide the factor set for measurement and so give a basis for the judgements which have to be made as to the measures which can be applied to each CSF to monitor progress in the area. The measures are therefore selected in accordance with their relevance to the established goals. Although they are typically diverse in nature (financial, non-financial, quantitative, qualitative, objective, and subjective) they do share the characteristic of relevance to the achievement of the particular objectives in question.

Figure 4.6 outlines the CSF approach framework and illustrates how the system generates a reasonably sized package of measures which (a) are derived from the goals which are being pursued and (b) can be designed to relate to various types of business or segments within the business.

The Balanced Scorecard

The idea of a Balanced Scorecard was introduced by Robert Kaplan of the Harvard Business School as an attempt to integrate traditional financial performance measures with contemporary qualitative measures. The Balanced Scorecard endorses the view that financial statement information and analysis are still essential for evaluating current operating performance and should not be abandoned. However, it recognises that to avoid the pitfalls of these measures they need to be supplemented with qualitative indicators that measure longer-term performance.

Based on Kaplan's research, four perspectives of corporate performance have been highlighted which comprise the Balanced Scorecard:

1.   **Financial.** Measures performance with respect to creating value for the shareholders.

2.   **Customers.** Measures performance with respect to adding value for existing and new customers.

3.   **Internal.** Measures performance with respect to operations and processes to achieve corporate objectives.

4.   **Innovation Learning.** Measures performance with respect to improvement, and creating future value.

		COMPANY (Overtrading Scenario)		COMPANY (Growth Scenario)		R & D Dept		MANUFACTURING WORK CELL
GOALS:		EPS growth ROI growth		EPS growth ROI growth		New Product Creation New Production Process Creation		Work to capacity Eliminate defects
CRITICAL SUCCESS FACTORS:	1	Credit Control	1	Stockmarket Profile	1	Hiring/retention of staff	1	Machine Reliability
	2	Stock Control	2	New Product Development	2	Liaison with Production/Marketing	2	Labour Availability
	3	Cost Control	3	Geographical Coverage	3	Volume and Cost effectiveness of new developments	3	Employee Morale
	4	Customer	4	Pricing Policy	4	Novelty/Innovation of new ideas	4	Supply Reliability
PERFORMANCE MEASURES:	1	Number of Days Credit	1	P/E ratio Analyst Reports	1	Number of job applicants	1	Throughput ratio Capacity
		Amount of Bad Depts				Labour Turnover Rates		Preventative maintenance expenditure
	2	Number of Days Stock	2	Number of new product launches	2	Surveys of production/ marketing personnel views	2	Labour Turnover Training Time
		Lead Time of Manufacture				Number of join seminars held		
	3	Profit Margins Cost Variances	3	Number of Agencies Location of new Agencies	3	Number of new product launches	3	Days Absent Attitude Survey
	4	Repeat Orders Customer Attitudes	4	Price differential versus competitors Sales Value Growth	4	Number of patents obtained Royalty income	4	Late Deliveries Returns

Figure 4.6 The critical success factor framework.

These four perspectives can help management formulate the set of performance measures that balance short-term financial performance with long-term non-financial measures. Financial measures, such as cash flow, turnover, and return on investment, are useful indicators for measuring short-term financial return. However continued success depends on balancing this with other factors. For example, from the perspective of maintaining customer satisfaction, measures such as the percentage of sales from new customers, on-time deliveries, and amount of support services, are valuable indicators of progress and success. In addition, internal operational measures such as cycle time, unit costs, and cost variance analysis are necessary for evaluating the performance of the processes established to meet customer demand. However indicators are not only needed to measure how well the business is currently achieving operational demands, also relevant is its future potential. Indicators such as percentage of sales from new products, engineering to market speed, and research and development output rates, are necessary for measuring the likelihood of continued future success.

Kaplan's studies of companies using the Balanced Scorecard approach reveal that it is being used not just as a measurement system, but rather as a central management system for the organisation. In one case the scorecard was used to translate the mission and strategic objectives of the firm into operational measures that employees could use to guide their day-to-day behaviour. In another case, it was used to unify strategic planning and operational budgeting processes, which were previously considered to be virtually unconnected.

Although each organisation is unique, and must devise measures suitable for their own specific industry and environment, Kaplan has suggested that implementation of the Balanced Scorecard should follow seven general steps:

1. **Preparation.** The organisation must define an appropriate business unit, preferably one which has its own customers, distribution channels, and production facilities.

2. **Initial Interviews.** Executives and shareholders are interviewed to gain insight into the company's mission and objectives in order to frame a proposal for a set of performance measures.

3. **Top Executive Workshop: First round.** A top management team works together, debating the proposed mission and objectives until a consensus is reached. It then formulates a preliminary Balanced Scorecard containing operational measures designed to fulfil the strategic objectives. Each member of the team is normally interviewed after the documents and output of the workshop have been concluded.

4. **Middle Manager Workshop.** Another workshop is used to gather together middle managers, who have an opportunity to debate the performance measurement proposals formulated by top management. In addition, an implementation plan is normally developed at this stage.

5.   **Top Executive Workshop:** Second round. A second executive workshop is conducted to consider the input of middle managers, and to formulate a final version of the scorecard. The team then agrees on the implementation plan, communicating the scorecard to employees, integrating it into the corporate culture, and developing the information system to support it.

6.   **Implementation.** Implementing the scorecard plan involves linking the performance measures with databases and information systems, and setting up a system for distribution and feedback of system results.

7.   **Periodic Reviews.** System results should be collected and reported regularly, and serve as a basis for management discussion and review. Normally, the scorecard metrics are revisited annually, as part of the strategic planning process.

The Balanced Scorecard thus is designed to join the strategic vision of the company with the day-to-day behaviour of its employees. It operationalises strategy into a set of performance measures that can be used to guide actions and solve problems. The Balanced Scorecard is therefore consistent with new management initiatives which foster cross-functional integration with Business Process Re-engineering, and with policies of continuous improvement. It is a tool that links together long-term performance measures with short-term tactical manoeuvres, balancing the perspective of management and resulting in improved decisions.

5 Improving performance I - costing techniques

Introduction

This chapter comprises a review of how one subset of management accounting, costing, can be designed to produce information which will assist management in improving the performance of their organisation. Three approaches to costing are reviewed. The first, activity based cost management, has the potential to direct attention and guid decision-making by providing new and innovative perspectives on how resources have been consumed. The second, quality costing, complements the quest for enhancement of output quality and the third, life cycle costing, supports the longer-term perspective in product oriented planning.

Activity Based Cost Management

Activity based costing (ABC) rose to prominence in the late 1980s from a series of Harvard business case studies based on leading USA corporations and authored by Robin Cooper, and Robert Kaplan. Thus originally ABC was developed by practitioners in these USA firms to improve cost information. The results of the ABC approach contrasted with traditional product costing methods, revealing some systematic differences in product costs. These were attributable to the traditional approaches primarily using direct labour hours to allocate overhead costs to products. However, as the use of direct labour hours had become a smaller part of the total costs in most manufacturing companies, it had become a less reliable indicator of cost behaviour. It was no longer simply direct labour that was driving the key elements of modern manufacturing costs, but rather a range of factors related to product complexity, quality and diversity. ABC addressed this problem by building a range of factors relating to product complexity, quality and diversity into the costing. Both ABC and traditional costing systems contain a two stage process, but differ with respect to how resources are allocated. This difference is shown in Figure 5.1.

The traditional approach focuses on functional departments, such as Finance, Production, Marketing, and Engineering. In the first stage costs are allocated to functional areas, then, in the second stage, direct labour or another output volume based measure is used as a basis for allocating functional factory overhead costs to each individual product. In contrast, ABC focuses on activities and related business processes which often cross the boundaries of functional departments (see Figure 5.4 below). It therefore shows how resources have been used within the organisation. In the first stage, costs are traced to the activities that are performed in the organisation. Then in the second stage, activity costs are traced to the products using numerous different cost drivers. In essence an ABC system is designed in accord with the structure shown in Figure 5.2.

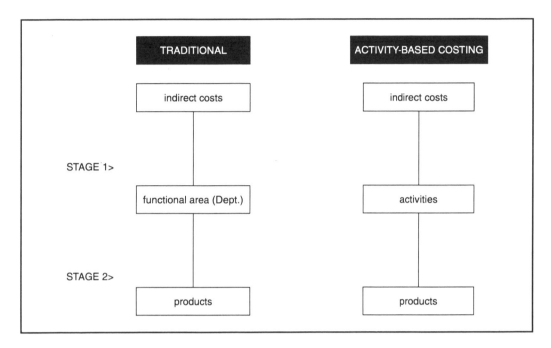

Figure 5.1 Two stage systems compared.

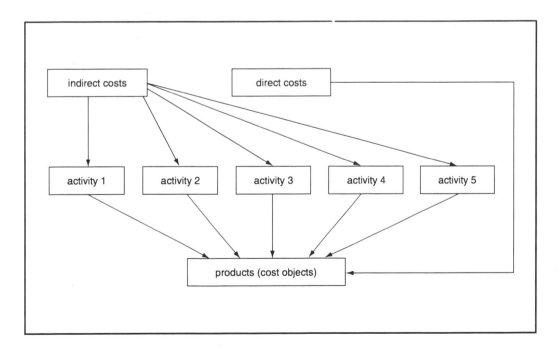

Figure 5.2 Activity-based costing model.

Direct material and direct labour are normally traced directly to the cost objects (normally products) through material and time sheet documentation. So an ABC system is really only concerned with indirect costs, the area of cost which has mushroomed to support enhanced quality, complexity and diversity. In the first stage of the ABC process, indirect resources are traced to specific activities performed in the organisation using appropriate cost drivers. A range of cost drivers are used again in the second stage of the process to trace activity costs to the final cost object. The components of the system are defined in detail below.

Resource. A resource is an expense category in the ledger. It can also be a group of expense categories that have a homogeneous cost behaviour pattern known as a cost pool. Examples of resources are rent expense, salaries and wages, depreciation expense, and utilities expense.

Activity. An activity is basically any significant aspect of organisational work that is directed at fulfilling a company objective. An activity name can also be used to represent a group of activities with similar objectives known as activity centres. Activity names are normally expressed in action terms, such as processing purchase orders, inspecting materials, performing credit checks, preparing financial statements, and loading part into machine. Care should be taken to ensure that the activity name is linked to the mission of the firm, and is objective, measurable, observable, and processual in nature. The composition of activities depends on the organisation, its industry, complexity of the product, and how it achieves its objectives. They can be described in great detail, or in broad terms. There is no set of activities that can be prescribed: activity definition is an introspective process, depending on management's agenda and, perspective, and the purpose given to the system.

Cost Driver. A cost object is essentially an operational transaction which links resources to activities and activity costs to cost objects. It is a tool that allocates costs through the ABC system based on a cause-and-effect principle. Unlike the traditional approach, ABC makes use of multiple cost drivers, which are intended to serve as a cause-and-effect link between resources and activities, and between activities and cost objects. In the first stage, cost drivers are normally referred to as activity drivers, as their purpose is to represent how the activities consume resources. In the second stage, cost drivers are used again to represent how cost objects consume activities, and are therefore referred to as resource drivers. Examples of cost drivers might include the number of purchase orders, the number of engineering changes, direct labour hours, machine hours, number of telephone calls, and number of batch set-ups. There are no standard set of cost drivers. Again, the selection depends on how best to express a cause-and-effect link.

Cost Object. A cost object is anything that management desires to know the value of in terms of cost. Cost objects are normally work outputs such as the different products or services that a company offers to its customers, but they may also be distribution channels, markets segments, internal processes, and customers.

Examples of each term are presented in Figure 5.3.

RESOURCES	ACTIVITIES	COST DRIVERS	COST OBJECT
utilities expense advertising expense production wages depreciation expense interest expense freight expense cost of materials administrative salaries data processing salaries payroll taxes	processing purchase orders processing accounts payable receiving materials maintaining the facility preparing sales forecasts counting inventory handling customer complaints testing for product defects making sales calls loading materials into machine	number of PO line items number of stock room transfers number of labour hours number of complaints number of batch set ups for production sales volume number of units produced number of engineering changes square footage number of stock transfers	product line service distribution client market segment customer

Figure 5.3 Examples of ABC.

The traditional costing approach is based on a vertical look at the organisation with each functional area as a vertical boundary line. In contrast, ABC is a horizontal slice through an organisation passing through many functional areas. Thus by tracing costs to activities, a process view of the organisation is revealed. Activities are performed both in and across functional areas. It therefore reflects the reality of how business work processes operate and avoids adherence to the often arbitrary divisions of the formal organisation chart. ABC reflects the fact that functional departments are interrelated with interconnecting activities that cross functional boundaries, requiring extensive coordination. For example, consider the material handling activity presented in Figure 5.4.

The process of handling materials involves coordinating activities from four different departments. The purchasing department has to order the right quantity of goods at the right time. The receiving department has to accept these goods and ensure that the order is accurate and complete. The inventory department stores the materials in an orderly manner to allow for systematic use in the production department. Viewing the organisation horizontally across functional boundaries helps management focus on processes, enabling better coordination between functional areas. Furthermore a knowledge of the cost analysed by activity rather than department provides a clear profile of why and how resources have been consumed within the firm. Not only does this information help in costing outputs but it provides a basis for assessing and managing costs (see Figure 5.5).

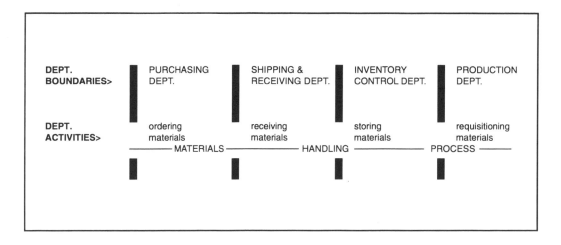

Figure 5.4 Horizontal view of the firm provided by ABC – Material Handling Activity

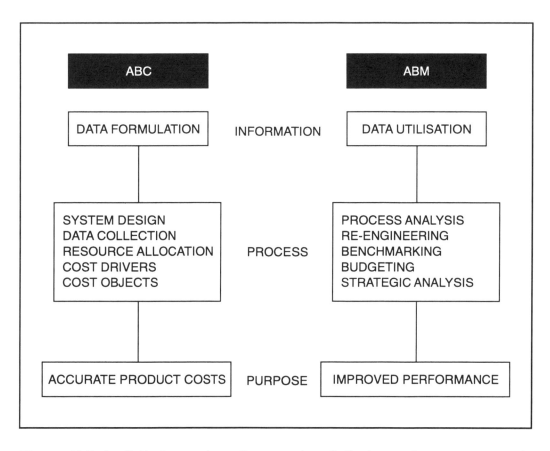

Figure 5.5 Activity-based costing and activity-based management.

ABM uses activity information to improve operational performance. ABC refers to the development of activity information and ABM refers to the utilisation of that information to improve the way the business operates. ABM is used for analysing processes and activities, re-engineering, benchmarking, budgeting, and strategic analysis. ABM gives cost visibility by showing how resources are used and by linking activities to them. It helps management answer two fundamental questions:

1.   How costs are incurred

2.   How to change costs

Activity Based Cost Management

(1) Understanding Cost Behaviour

ABC extends the traditional concept that all cost behaviour should be categorised with respect only to output volume (fixed, variable or semi-variable). From an ABC perspective, all costs are variable depending upon their cost driver. Volume is only one cost driver among many possibilities. Certainly direct materials and direct labour may mainly be driven by volume but there are a variety of different costs hidden within the classification of overhead that are primarily fixed with respect to volume but are variable in relation to an appropriate cost driver. Cooper has argued that cost variability could be classified using four major hierarchical groups bridging the fixed/variable dichotomy:

1.   **Unit-based.** Cost variation occurs in proportion to production volume.

2.   **Batch-based.** Cost variation occurs in proportion to the number of batches in the production process. Scheduling and set-up activities are driven at this level.

3.   **Product-based.** Cost variation occurs in proportion to product type and design changes. Resourcing, scheduling of quality and procurement activities are driven at this level.

4.   **Facility-based.** Cost variation occurs in proportion to changes in the general facility. These costs are generally considered fixed and only change if facility adjustments are made.

This hierarchical approach to cost variation is intended to provide a realistic extension to the traditional highly simplistic fixed/variable categorisation when modelling cost. However, in order to view this new concept of variability, we have to go beyond costs in their raw form and look at them in their new more revealing activity form. So when we speak of cost behaviour in an ABC context we are referring not to cost categories or expenses, but rather to activity costs. Some activity costs will be fixed in relation to the number of units produced, but variable in respect of some other cost variation base. For example, the cost of the activity of processing purchase orders may be relatively fixed in relation to the number of units produced, but variable to the number of purchase orders and number of supplies used. In other words, cost variability is best expressed in terms of the appropriate cost driver.

(2) Cost Control

The information generated by an ABC system also supports the managerial analysis of costs for control and reduction of purposes. For example, consider a manager who is given the following cost information about purchasing activity in the firm from the requisite general ledger accounts:

LEDGER EXPENSES: PURCHASING	Current Month	Budget for the Month
Salaries	£290	£295
Office equipment – Depreciation	84	84
Travel expenses	158	145
Office supplies	31	24
Telephone expense	29	15
	------	------
Total monthly expenses	£592	£563

This is typical information found in traditional costing systems. Departmental managers are asked to use this information to either try to reduce costs or find a more productive way of doing things. But how does a manager use this information to improve the department? The manager might be given last year's monthly budget to compare and then maybe focus on the costs that have increased the most. Perhaps he/she notices that the telephone expense appears to be too high, and consequently instructs the staff to cut down on phone calls. This is the extent of the initiative. It is very difficult to try to make cuts and improve the productivity of the department based solely on this financial information. Analysing this data does not provide answers to where or why waste and inefficiencies might exist. Management needs to know where to focus their efforts and ABC can provide such guidance.

Suppose that the company has implemented an ABC system and the purchasing manager receives the following activity information about the department:

PURCHASING: ACTIVITY INFORMATION	Monthly
Checking customer credit	89
Taking a customer order	103
Collecting pricing information	120
Customer communications	58
Solving order problems	95
Answering customer questions	25
Preparing purchase orders	102
Total monthly expenses	£592

Notice that the same amount of total costs remain assigned to purchasing, but are now represented in activity form rather than resource input form. Consider how activity information can focus attention to help management reduce costs and increase efficiency. The purchasing manager might notice that a lot of resources are devoted to solving problems. Other questions arise: What kind of problems are occurring? Are these problems caused by products or internal processes? Could we change the way we do things to either reduce the problems or find a better way of addressing them? The other thing to notice is that the highest activity cost is collecting pricing information. Why does this activity consume so much of the department's resources? Why is the pricing information not easily obtainable? This problem could be looked into further. It may turn out that pricing information has not been organised or that discounting policies have not been established. In addition, this may be why telephone costs are so high. One can see that having activity information provides visibility to enhance cost control and manage the activities which consume resources within the firm.

Activity Based Budgetary Analysis

The cost reduction aspects of activity analysis can be extended to budget planning. At the budget setting stage activity resource requirements can be expressed both in monetary terms and in cost driver transaction terms. Combining these aspects of resource consumption gives a more complete view of cost behaviour for budgeting purposes. For example, a budget figure of £25,000 may be set at the beginning of the fiscal year for the activity of managing customer queries. The monetary figure is based on expected cost driver transactions of 5,000 queries. If cost variances result, the number of cost driver transactions could be examined to determine if the increase, or decrease, in expense is justified with respect to the changes in the volume of work. A standard productivity measure could be established based on the expected costs per unit of cost driver. For example, the standard cost for managing customer queries would be £5 (£25,000/5,000) per customer query. If the cost of the resources consumed by the activity increases and the number of cost driver occurrences stays the same or declines, this may be an indication that productivity has been reduced.

Traditional budget variance analysis could be constructed using activity-based information. However, in contrast to traditional approaches, Activity-Based Budgeting (ABB) gives added visibility to the cost variance and provides a more constructive signal for investigation. Visibility is enhanced by showing how overhead resources are used. The variance is segmented by activities which can also be broken down into spending and usage variances. For example, consider the example above of managing customer queries. The variances for this activity are shown in Figure 5.6 below.

COST INFORMATION:

    (SR) STANDARD RATE (£25,000/5,000) = £5 PER QUERY
    (SQ) STANDARD USAGE = 5,000 QUERIES
    BUDGETED COST = £25,000
    (AQ) ACTUAL USAGE = 4,000 QUERIES
    ACTUAL COST = £28,000
    (AR) ACTUAL RATE (£28,000/4,000) = £7 PER QUERY

SPENDING VARIANCE: (AQ X (SR - AR))

    4,000 X (£5 - £7) = £8,000 UNFAVOURABLE

USAGE VARIANCE: ((SR X (SQ - AQ))

    £5 X (5,000 - 4,000) = £5,000 UNFAVOURABLE

Figure 5.6 Managing queries variance analysis.

The usage variance indicates the level of operating capacity of the activity. The activity-based usage variance indicates that, for the period under examination, the activity of managing queries is at 80% (4,000/5,000) of capacity. However, in terms of resources, the level of resource consumption is in excess of capacity by 112% (£28,000/£25,000). This analysis indicates a reduction in the level of productivity for this activity of 40% ((£7 − £5)/£5). Therefore, an investigation of why the standard is not being achieved should be undertaken.

Capacity Analysis

The assignment of capacity to an activity is much more complex than simply determining the expected cost and driver levels. Activities are composed of a myriad of resource expense categories. The activity may have both committed and flexible resources traced to it. Flexible resources are supplied only as needed, and no unused capacity exists. In contrast, committed resources are supplied (as a service stock) in advance of usage and consequently can result in excess capacity existing. The committed resource portion should have a different cost driver and level of capacity than the flexible portion of the activity cost. The flexible cost driver depicts the rate of resource consumption in direct proportion to resource spending. In contrast, the cost driver used for the committed cost portion of the activity cost will exhibit an indirect relationship between usage and spending. This two tier approach could be used to apply ABB concepts. For example, manufacturing equipment and factory floor space may be dedicated to the activity of inspections. In this case, two different cost drivers are required to assign resource expenses to cost objects. The committed expenses (equipment and space) are assigned, based on the capacity or expected capabilities provided by these resources, while the expenses of the flexible resources (inspectors) are assigned, based on the activity volumes actually realised. This procedure for committed expenses is consistent with the traditional approach of using normal activity levels for overhead absorption.

Attribute Labelling

Activity cost attributes can be applied to activities to enhance cost visibility. Attributes are qualitative descriptions of costs that increase the usability of the cost information to make operational decisions. Many companies that have implemented ABC have found it useful to add qualitative variables to activities to bring out hidden information capable of improving the production process. Traditionally, the dichotomy of fixed and variable have been attributes which attempt to further describe a cost. ABC takes this process of description further by suggesting that multiple labels can be used to enhance cost visibility. The most popular of these is the value and non-value-added attribute. Companies found it useful to label activities in terms of the value that each contributes to the organisation. Activities that involve correcting, checking, and reworking are normally seen as activities that add little value. Activities classified as non-value added can be targeted for cost reduction or elimination, and high value activities can be supported and promoted. Other attribute labels include the following:

1.   Committed and non-committed costs

2.   Sunk costs, variable, fixed, and mixed

3.   Controllable and non-controllable

4.   Discretionary and non-discretionary

In addition, other attribute coding schemes have been used. For example, some companies have found it useful to assign reason-codes to activities to provide insight as to why the activity is performed in the first place. Also purpose codes have been used to help management determine if the activity is supportive to the corporate mission. Finally process codes can also be attached to activities to indicate which process the activity supports, and provide clues to help coordinate with other activities.

Limitations

There are some limitations to ABC. For example, in theory, ABC only works if the cost driver used to represent the consumption of a resource has a positive linear correlation with the cost. This is a very strict condition, and most ABC systems are likely to fail if this requirement were stringently applied. However in practice it is not necessary for this condition to be perfectly met if the philosophy that it is better to be approximately correct than absolutely wrong is adopted. ABC should not be based on strict mathematical or econometric criteria, but rather on the usefulness that can be derived from applying it in practice. One prominent critic of full costing systems has been Goldratt who has argued that preoccupation with costs detracts from the money making objective of business. He has suggested that the Theory of Constraints (see Chapter 6) provides more appropriate information to guide management. Other problems with the theory of ABC include the following:

1.   The premise that activities cause costs cannot be validated. For example, decisions and the passage of time may be the real underlying causes of costs. Claiming a single cause is too simplistic and misleading.

2.   A change in activity would not necessarily result in a change in costs. For example, there may be reductions in an activity without any changes to expenses. That is, productivity improvement can be made, but only managerial decisions to cut spending can result in cost reductions.

Current Practice

Again the vailidity of these criticisms can be tested by assessing the real-world use of the approach. For example in practice activity information may trigger the decisions which result in cost changes and in this respect it is of value. Innes and Mitchell's 1995 survey of the largest UK companies reveals that ABC is used and applied in many areas of management accounting including pricing, decision making, cost reduction, budgeting, product design, customer profitability analysis, and performance measurement. The results indicate that ABC is currently used in a significant number of companies in the UK, and is being assessed in many more. Comparing some of the data of the latest Innes and Mitchell survey with earlier surveys indicates a significant increase in the number of firms using and considering ABC. Almost 20% of the companies surveyed were reported to be using some form of ABC, while another 27% were in the process of considering it. Over half of the companies either had rejected using ABC or had never considered it. Most of the respondents who used ABC reported applying it primarily towards cost reduction efforts and performance measurement.

Relating to the companies considering the implementation of ABC, the survey results indicate that the most significant expected benefit of adopting ABC was its ability to make costs visible which would assist in controlling overhead costs. The firms rejecting the use of ABC emphasised the high costs associated with implementing and maintaining the system. Other reasons included satisfaction with the current cost management system and a lack of perceived benefits from ABC.

Where is ABC Appropriate?

So what is the appropriate environment for an ABC system? If product variation is low then a traditional volume based costing system may provide a reasonably accurate product cost. However, if different products in a single organisation consume resources at different rates due to differences in product complexity and diversity in marketing, production, and distribution, an ABC system may result in more accurate product costs. ABC systems are most appropriate when four factors are present:

Factor 1: When competition is high. The benefits of ABC can be most appreciated in a highly competitive market. When market competition is high, intense pressure is placed on pricing policy which creates a need for more accurate costing tools. In addition, margins may be increased by increasing the price of some products while new market share could be captured by reducing the price on other products. Possessing accurate product cost in a competitive environment provides the basic tools for product strategy, positioning, and promotion.

Factor 2: When product mix is diverse. A singular cost allocation method, such as direct labour, is unlikely to capture accurate product costs when product mix is diverse in terms of batch sizes, physical size, raw materials, and the degree of complexity. ABC systems allow for multiple cost drivers which could be tailored to represent different aspects of each product composition. By using activities and multiple cost drivers to trace cost to products, there is likely to be less distortion than with traditional costing systems.

Factor 3: When indirect costs are a significant proportion of total cost. Under these circumstances the propensity of ABC to improve costing is greater. In these circumstances the overhead context of product or service cost has the potential to materially influence the set of unit costs produced by the costing system. Of course this effect will also be more pronounced where the content of overhead reflects the existence of complexity and diversity in the operations of the firm.

Factor 4: When the transaction environment is computerised. ABC is highly reliant on electronic data processing equipment to collect and manipulate large amounts of information. In organisations where operations, transactions, and accounting information are highly automated, activity based information is more efficiently captured and utilised in an ABC system.

Using activity information to manage costs adds a new and interesting dimension to management and management accounting. The range of applications of ABM demonstrate that it is a significant and pervasive influence on cost management, and has the potential to contribute to a wide range of management decisions.

Cost of Quality

Total Quality Management (TQM) is a system of management designed to anticipate, meet and exceed the customer's needs, wants, and expectations. It is a system intended to continually enhance both quality of product and service as well as quality of the workforce, employment, environment and any other aspect of the organization. The central thrust of TQM is a total commitment to quality throughout the organization with the ultimate goal being customer satisfaction. This new emphasis on quality is in contrast with traditional views as presented in Figure 5.7.

The old view of quality is that it has an inverse relationship with cost. The more you increase the quality of your product or service the more costs will be incurred. This is because traditionally the way quality was increased was by placing more effort on inspection, testing and monitoring. The modern TQM view is that increasing quality actually lowers costs because defects and inspection costs are reduced. The trend now is away from 'inspecting-in' quality towards 'building-in' quality. Rather than try to catch all the defective product before it reaches the customer, management should try to improve the production process so that less defects occur in the first place.

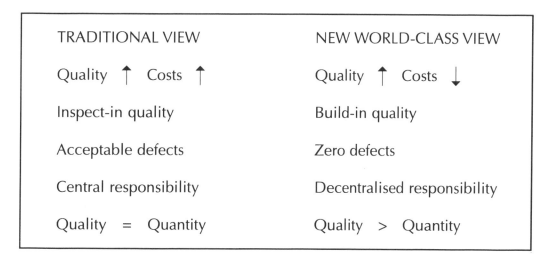

Figure 5.7 TQM compared to traditional view on quality.

Traditionally, management has accepted defects as a natural phenomenon. It was typical for a standard percentage of defects and waste to be a normal part of the production process. However, potentially inspired by the Japanese, companies are finding out that smaller and smaller percentages of defects are possible with zero defects being the goal. Progress in this respect can be enhanced by pursuing TQM policy and supporting it with the costing analysis which indicates its economic viability.

1.   **Top Management Commitment.** Gaining top management support is the essential first step in implementing a TQM programme. Senior executives must provide leadership and financial capital, encouraging the entire organisation to focus on the TQM initiative.

2.   **Quality Oriented Company Culture.** Quality is everyone's business, and each person in the organisation needs to be motivated to perform activities that contribute to a quality product or service. Quality must become a way of life.

3.   **Measure It.** Management must construct quality measurements to determine whether or not their actions are resulting in higher levels of quality. Key quality indicators should be identified and transformed into reliable measures to provide feedback about the TQM initiative.

4.   **Base Performance on Quality.** Just as organisational members are rewarded for taking actions that result in higher sales, they must also be rewarded for contributions to quality. Therefore, performance should be tied to quality indicators to motivate people to perform their jobs in a way that enhances the quality of the organisation and products.

Application of these principles as a practical policy requires a phased plan of implementation:

Phase 1: Determine quality attributes. Quality attributes are qualitative expressions of essential aspects of a quality product or service. For example, quality attributes for a bakery might include freshness, good taste, fast service, and friendly atmosphere.

Phase 2: Identify quality attribute determinants. Determinants are the key factors that are necessary for achieving a particular attribute. For example, the attribute determinant for 'fast service' in a bakery might be 'time'.

Phase 3: Establish economical and objective control measures. An economical measures is one that cost less than the expected benefit that it provides. An objective measure is one that can be relied upon and is free from bias and manipulation. For example, a economical and objective measure of the attribute determinant 'time' might be the span between the moment the customer enters the store to the time he/she is exits the store.

Phase 4: Develop quality indicators. Once an objective measure is established, it needs to be transformed into a quantifiable indicator that faithfully represents changes in the quality attribute. For example, an indicator of fast delivery could be measured by dividing the number of customers serviced in a given day by the total hours the store was inhabited by customers.

A summary of this process, using a bakery as an example, is presented below:

PHASE 1 Quality attributes	PHASE 2 Attribute	PHASE 3 Measure	PHASE 4 Indicator
Fast service	time	enter-exit period	– No of customers – in store time

You could stand at the bakery door all day with a stop-watch and record the time for each and every customer, but this likely to cost too much. So the question arises, should companies blindly pursue quality or should they consider the costs as well as the benefits? There are 4 different types of quality costs that should be considered when implementing a quality program:

1. **Prevention costs.** Prevention costs are the costs incurred to prevent poor quality. This may be considered the smallest cost with the largest potential benefit. Examples include, training costs, security costs, design costs, and maintenance costs.

2. **Appraisal costs.** Appraisal costs are the costs incurred to identify non-conformity and monitoring of quality standards. Examples include, inspection costs, testing costs, supervision costs, and quality audits.

3. **Internal failure costs.** Internal failure costs are the costs incurred as a result of substandard processing quality. This includes the costs incurred to bring quality back to standard before it is sold to the customer. Examples include, rework costs, scrap costs, repair costs, down-time costs and retesting costs.

4. **External failure costs.** External failure costs are the costs incurred as a result of substandard raw materials or parts. This includes the costs to bring quality back to standard after it is sold to the customer. Examples include recall costs, warranty repair costs, and lost sales and customer costs.

A role for management accounting exists by developing quality indicators, and exposing costs associated with the attainment of quality in terms of appraisal costs, prevention costs, and internal and external failure costs. Financial viability of programmes can be assessed by comparing the trade-off from investing in class 1 and 2 costs and so reducing class 3 and 4 costs.

Life Cycle Costing

Life Cycle Costing (LCC) is a concept developed by the US Defense Department in the 1960s as a technique for evaluating the effectiveness of government procurement. However its broader application has attracted considerable interest in recent years. Traditional management accounting focuses primarily on the production stage of product development. Product costs such as design costs, marketing costs, training costs and research and development costs, although significant, are not extensively integrated into product cost calculations nor are they regularly subject to the normal financial control process set up to monitor production activity. LCC considers the costs of a product during its entire life from initial design to final withdrawal from the market place. It therefore emphasises that management accounting can be applied at every stage of the product life cycle not just after production has occurred. The traditional view of accounting for product costs can be contrasted with LCC in the following manner presented in Figure 5.8.

	TRADITIONAL VIEW	**LIFE CYCLE VIEW**
Responsibility:	Accounting function	Organisational function
Cost behaviour:	Static cost	Dynamic cost
Product life:	Production phase	All phases
Cost treatment:	Period costs	Averaged costs

Figure 5.8 Life cycle costing vs. traditional costing.

The traditional view of product costing is that it is an accounting function based mainly on production costs. In contrast, LCC considers other functional departments such as marketing, engineering, distribution, and purchasing to have equal responsibility. The LCC view is that product costs are incurred not just in the production process, but also in the design and marketing processes as well. Consequently, product costing becomes an organisational function, incorporating a wider organisational perspective on product development. Traditionally, once product costs are determined, the cost remains basically static unless production inputs change. LCC offers a dynamic view of product costs. It considers that product costs change as a product moves from one stage of the product life cycle to the next. For example, in the early stages research and design costs are incurred, while production costs and sales revenue are insignificant. Therefore, a product could be said to have different costs depending upon the stage of development.

This approach is particularly relevant for new product development. Studies have shown that as much as 80% of the total cost of a product is committed even before it reaches production. LCC highlights the need for the management accountant to be involved in the early stages of the product life cycle when crucial cost commitment decisions are being made. It is at this stage that management accounting techniques can have a really significant effect in influencing cost (see for example the performance improvement techniques reviewed in Chapter 6). Moreover recognising that costs are dynamic and change over the product's life is inconsistent with the generally accepted practice of treating research and development, and advertising costs as period costs to be written off when incurred. LCC does not necessarily endorse capitalising these costs; rather it suggests that they should be considered over all phases of a product's life when profitability evaluations and pricing decisions are made.

The life cycle view is that every product has five stages of life, and at each stage different aspects of product costs are incurred. The 5 stages are as follows:

Stage 1: Pre-Introduction. The pre-introduction stage is where research and development occur, and where prototypes are conceived. At this stage design, testing, and planning costs peak, declining as the product matures.

Stage 2: Introduction. The introduction stage is where the product is actually launched into the market place. At this stage marketing, advertising and promotion costs are at their highest point.

Stage 3: Growth. If the product is successfully introduced into the market place and accepted by its target customers, the growth period begins. Sales and profits begin to rise dramatically, and unit costs decline as volume increases. Most of the costs at this stage are concerned with distribution, and sustaining customer loyalty. In addition, total production costs begin to rise as more raw materials and labour are used to achieve larger unit volumes.

Stage 4: Maturity. The maturity stage is where the product experiences market saturation. Sales and profits level off. The company either begins to replace the product or significantly updates the current one. Therefore, at this stage the firm needs to decide whether to initiate further research and development costs or allow for new products already in the pipeline to take over.

Stage 5: Decline. The decline stage is marked by falling sales and profit margins, and new competing products are gaining market share. At this stage plans are being made to abandon the product, requiring disposal costs such as the selling-off of obsolete inventory, cessation of production operations, selling of production facilities, and termination of labour resources.

Not all products will exhibit every stage nor will they occur at the same rate. Some very well known successful products have stayed in the maturity stage for decades. It also depends on the particular type of industry. For example, the product life cycles for high technology products seem to be getting increasingly shorter, while those for heavy industrial machinery products remain relatively long in comparison.

Viewing a product in terms of its life cycle can lead to interesting changes in the organisation, particularly where the assessment involves multi-disciplinary teams. Traditionally, functional departments contributed their expertise independently of other functions in the company. For example, in the early stages of a product's life the engineering department may design a technically superior product in record time without giving consideration to the potential difficulties which may arise when the product is actually produced on the plant floor. The production department is then forced to build a product within certain cost constraints and specifications which may not be entirely feasible given the current design. Thus the full interrelationship of decisions and costs are made explicit and product worth is comprehensively evaluated under the LCC approach.

6 Improving performance II – other techniques

Introduction

This chapter reviews a further set of management accounting techniques which are dedicated to the enhancement of financial performance. They involve not only areas where cost reduction is possible but also the identification of opportunities where extra expenditure may produce extra value for the customer and may thus generate a more than compensating future income flow.

External Benchmarking

Benchmarking is a technique used by management to evaluate various internal performance measures of the firm against outside companies which possess a reputation for excellence. Comparisons can be drawn from other companies within the same industry, or with companies in other industries. By seeking benchmark comparitors from outside the industry, a company has an opportunity for a broader view of best practices, particularly in common activities such as accounting, purchasing and personnel. However, internal industry comparisons are likely to be more relevant for highlighting the strengths and weaknesses of core operational practice.

Financial measures are the most common form of information shared among companies in this way. This information typically includes financial ratios, and standard measures of efficiency and productivity. Measures such as expense-to-revenue ratios, return on assets (ROA), inventory turnover, revenue per employee can be supplemented by non-financial measures including service calls, customer satisfaction, and new product launches.

In order for a company to access benchmarking information from other companies, it normally has to join an intermediary organisation that serves as a clearing house for the collection and distribution of information. A high code of ethics is therefore necessary for conducting benchmarking studies, and proprietary or highly confidential information is not normally collected. Agreements and assurances with regard to security and anonymity are often prerequisites for companies joining a benchmarking organisation. Other less systematic sources of benchmarking information can come from inspecting trade journals, advertising brochures, annual reports, company visits, new staff and management consultants.

Benchmarking Focus

Benchmarking initiatives can focus on strategic, functional or operational performance. Strategic benchmarking measures are concerned with the position the company has relative to its competitors. Examples of strategic performance measures include market share, profit margins, leverage, and return on investment (ROI). While strategic benchmarks are derived for competitor information generally at the overall company level, functional benchmarks are non-competitor-based information about specific functional areas of the company. For example, a functional benchmarking initiative might seek to compare the engineering department or the purchasing department with non-computer companies who have established reputations for excellence in these particular functional areas. Examples of functional benchmarking measures could be the number of engineering changes, speed of order delivery, and cost per purchase order. Operational benchmarking is usually performed at the activity or task level. Here the focus is on specific activities within functional areas. An example of an operational benchmarking measure might be to compare the activity of making sales visits to customers. The performance indicator for evaluating this activity could be the average number of visits required before a sale is obtained. All or any of these types of benchmarking may be appropriate to an organisation intent on improving performance.

One problem with benchmarking is that it tends to limit management's thinking to what has 'already been done' as opposed to 'what could be done'. Aspiring only to be as good as the best in the industry sets artificial limits on innovation and improvement. Benchmarking information may therefore be used merely as a tool for catching-up, rather than for surpassing industry standards. Benchmarking can, however, generate innovative ideas, particularly when it compares practices with companies outside the industry. The Xerox Corporation used benchmarking to compare itself to a clothes distribution company (L.L. Bean Ltd.). As a result of examining the warehousing and distribution practices of this company, Xerox claims to have improved productivity by 3% to 5%.

Implementation

Implementing a benchmarking programme requires a significant amount of time, effort, and money. This often necessitates top management leadership and support. The implementation process can be formalised into five distinct phases:

1.   **Planning.** The benchmarking process must be planned to identify and prioritise which aspects of the company are to be focused

upon. In addition, the plan must clarify who the intended users will be of the information. Normally a benchmarking team is assembled to formulate the benchmarking plan, defining performance indicators and methods for collecting information.

2. **Data Gathering.** Collecting benchmarking information involves research and cooperation. Research is necessary to collect information that is unavailable through benchmarking organisations. This is accomplished through the analysis of trade journals, company reports, advertisements, and questioning of suppliers, salespersons, and customers. In order to gain access to information provided by benchmarking organisations, compliance with certain procedures and protocol is necessary.

3. **Analysis.** The benchmarking measures collected must be compared with internal performance measures in order to determine where a gap in performance exists. However, it is normally necessary to make certain adjustments to the performance indicators in order to establish parity for accurate and reliable comparisons. Once areas that need improvement are identified, further analysis is needed to establish the causes of the performance gap, as well as possible avenues for closing the gap.

4. **Execution.** The benchmarking team must gain approval from senior management for the proposed actions which have been identified for closing the performance gap. Once approved, the actions are executed, and then evaluated. Progress must be assessed and objectives may have to be reformulated to adapt to changing conditions.

5. **Recalibration.** A system of feedback and control must be set up to inform management how effective the actions are in closing the performance gap. Performance indicators should be changed periodically to take into account changes in technology, previous success, and external events.

Through its capacity to initiate and direct change, benchmarking can make an important contribution to continuous improvement and total quality management. However, one of the most common pitfalls of benchmarking is identifying static performance targets and merely trying to copy the best practices from the other companies. The objective of benchmarking should be to provide realistic performance targets to help the company identify areas of weakness, focusing management efforts where they are needed most.

Theory of Constraints

The Theory of Constraints (TOC) is a theory of management based on the idea that every organisation has at least one constraint which prevents it from making money. Its focus is on reducing constraints and consequently increasing the throughput and moneymaking capacity of the business.

TOC was introduced by Eli Goldratt, an Israeli physicist. He asserts the goal of business is to make money both now and in the future. The key to this is the development of an ability to enhance the size and velocity of the flow of money within the firm. Three key variables affect the flow:

1.   **Throughput.** Money on its way to the system in the form of sales revenue after deducting material costs.

2.   **Inventory.** Money still in the system in the form of raw materials, work-in-process, and finished goods inventory.

3.   **Operating expense.** Money on its way out of the system in the form of expenses.

The TOC endorses a global view of efficiency regarding resource utilisation which contrasts with the traditional local view. Traditional approaches to resource utilisation focus on keeping every resource working as close to capacity as possible. Therefore, resources which operate at less than capacity are considered wasteful and inefficient. Moreover, an idle resource is unproductive and suppresses productivity. For example, if a production worker is seen sitting around, the supervisor's first inclination is to find him/her something to do. The idea is that each and every resource should be utilised to its capacity in order for the organisation as a whole to maximise its efficiency and hence its profitability.

TOC emphasises resource coordination over resource maximisation. From this perspective it is sometimes better to leave a resource idle if that state reduces inventory and does not impact on throughput. It distinguishes resource 'utilisation' from resource 'activation'. Resource activation is keeping the resource busy producing something. Resource utilisation is using the resource to make more money for the firm.

TOC has a throughput orientation, placing the highest priority on increasing throughput and reducing WIP inventory. Traditional management accounting has a cost orientation, placing operating cost control as its chief aim. The differences between TOC and the traditional view are summarised in Figure 6.1 below.

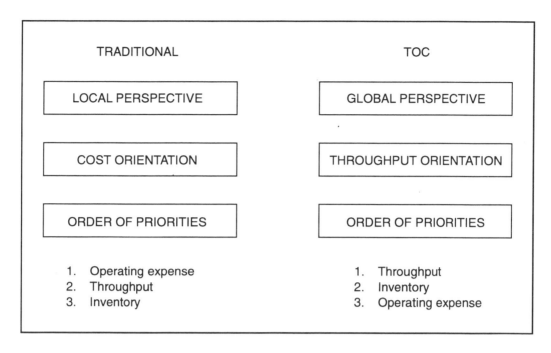

Figure 6.1 Traditional vs. TOC.

To illustrate differences between the local and global approach to efficiency, consider the following example. A simple manufacturing process uses two machines, Machine-A and Machine-B. Machine-A accepts raw materials and processes them further as input for Machine-B. Machine-B then processes a final product. The process and operational information is presented in Figure 6.2.

Raw Materials -------> Machine-A ----->Machine-B ---->Finished Product

MONTHLY STATISTICS
Standard capacity:	100 units	75 units
Actual production:	80 units	75 units
Standard unit costs:	£10	£8

Figure 6.2 Manufacturing process.

Given this information, where would you expect management to focus its attention? Traditional standard costing would direct management's attention to resources that have an unfavourable variance between capacity and usage. In this illustration, Machine-A results in an unfavourable variance because it is being underutilised. Capacity variances would be calculated as follows:

Machine-A: £10 x (100 - 80) = £200 unfavourable variance

Machine-B: £8 x (75 - 75) = 0

The variance analysis informs management that something must be done about Machine-A. To eliminate the waste, another 20 units need to be pushed through Machine-A. On the other hand, Machine-B is performing exactly as expected and requires no management attention. Suppose management is successful at eliminating the waste and bringing the actual production of Machine-A up to 100 units per month and thus eliminating the unfavourable variance. What would be the result to the organisation as a whole? In terms of standard costing, a significant improvement in productivity has been accomplished. Machine-A would not only now meet productivity expectations but the cost per unit would decline reflecting the elimination of unused capacity. Figure 6.3 presents production information that would result from operating the manufacturing process for 6 months with Machine-A and Machine-B both working at 100% of capacity.

Month	Units produced Mach-A	Mach-B	Cum. WIP units	Throughput in units
1	100	75	25	75
2	100	75	50	75
3	100	75	75	75
4	100	75	100	75
5	100	75	125	75
6	100	75	150	75

Figure 6.3 Maximising efficiency according to traditional approach.

Notice that improving the output of Machine-A to 100 units did not increase the level of throughput. This is because Machine-B is only able to process 75 units no matter how Machine-A performs. Also notice the accumulation of WIP inventory that results from pushing Machine-A to its capacity. So, even though variance analysis directed management to increase the output of Machine-A, no improvement in throughput has occurred. WIP inventory has increased and this will cause operating expense to increase as well. This problem develops from the fictional view that resources in the organisation are independent of each other and must be maximised to increase productivity.

TOC recognises that constraints or bottlenecks in the system govern the rate of throughput. A constraint is a factor of production that limits the profitability of an organisation. An example coule be a bottleneck resource such as a machine, a process, a department, a group of workers, or any other factor of production that is responsible for taking inputs and producing outputs. In the example above, Machine-B is the constraint because it determines the level of throughput. From a TOC perspective, it would be better to leave

Machine-A idle 25% of the time in order to minimise WIP and without reducing throughput. Figure 6.4 presents the results if management were no longer influenced by variance analysis and standard efficiency measures, only producing 75 units per month from Machine-A.

Month	Units produced Mach-A	Mach-B	Cum. WIP units	Throughput in units
1	75	75	0	75
2	75	75	0	75
3	75	75	0	75
4	75	75	0	75
5	75	75	0	75
6	75	75	0	75

Figure 6.4 Maximising efficiency according to TOC approach.

Notice that WIP does not accumulate while the rate of throughput is unaffected. So instead of focusing on resources performing at less than capacity, TOC directs management's attention to resources that need to operate at full capacity to maximise throughput. They act as the constraint on the system and determine the rate of throughput. According to TOC, in the example above, management should focus its efforts on Machine-B (the bottleneck) rather than Machine-A.

Concepts of Operation

TOC can be related to the Drum-Buffer-Rope concept. This suggests the resource constraints set the rhythm for the entire system. Since the bottleneck resource governs the rate of throughput, it should act as the 'drum-beat' setting the pace for the whole system. In addition, a bottleneck resource must be kept as busy as possible because production time lost on a bottleneck resource is throughput lost for the whole company. Therefore, a buffer of WIP inventory is normally essential for the bottleneck resource to accommodate fluctuations in work flow. The bottleneck resource also serves as the rope pulling production through the system. Rather than pushing the production process, the bottleneck determines the production rate for all non-bottleneck resources.

Implementing the TOC approach requires management to devise performance measures that specifically focus on throughput and the efficiency of bottleneck resources. The prime general measure of productivity is therefore as follows:

$$\text{Prime Measure} = \frac{\text{Throughput}}{\text{Total factory costs}}$$

Where the throughput is sales less material costs and total factory costs represent the cost of all other factors of production.

Moreover for individual bottlenecks alternative usage (e.g. in producing different product lines) requires to be based on throughput per unit of time for each use of the constraining resource. Management should attempt to balance the overall system with the capacity of the bottleneck resource, and in order to improve throughput they should continually attempt to break the bottleneck by offloading work elsewhere or by enhancing its capacity. Once a bottleneck is broken, another one takes its place in a different part of the system. Therefore, the TOC approach involves continually tracking and dealing with constraints in the organisation.

There are 4 general steps to implementing a TOC programme:

1.　　**Determine location of bottleneck resource.** A bottleneck resource can be found by noticing where WIP inventory is building-up. WIP inventory is likely to build-up just in front of the bottleneck resource.

2.　　**Optimise bottleneck resource.** Ensure that the bottleneck resource is kept busy. This can be done by using a strategic buffer of WIP in front of the bottleneck to accommodate fluctuations in demand. In addition, production processes can be redesigned to reduce the level of work required on the bottleneck. Bottlenecks can also be optimised by adding additional capacity.

3.　　**Operate non-bottleneck resources at bottleneck pace.** All non-bottleneck resources should be operated at less than their capacity to coordinate with the bottleneck resource and to minimise the build-up of WIP inventory.

4.　　**Monitor bottleneck efficiency.** Establish performance measures that focus on the bottleneck efficiency. If efficiency is improved to the point that excess capacity develops, the bottleneck has been broken and has moved elsewhere in the system. (Start again from 1 above.)

Although TOC has attracted a significant amount of interest, there are only a few documented examples of its use in practice. In terms of accounting TOC closely resembles traditional product contribution margin analysis. However,

Goldratt has brought new interest to the importance of the role of limiting factors on productivity which has been previously considered less significant. It also highlights the need to take a wider perspective on efficiency, one which reorients management's priorities from cost emphasis to a broader throughput emphasis.

Business Process Re-engineering

Business Process Re-engineering (BPR) is a technique which seeks to reconstruct the business processes upon which managerial and operational activity is based in order to increase efficiency and quality in a short period of time. BPR aims for performance 'breakthroughs', rather than incremental and continuous improvement advocated by Total Quality Management (TQM). In addition BPR focuses on cross-functional managerial operations, attempting to link together different activities between functional departments in a coordinated and streamlined process-flow.

In a survey of executives, 88% said that they have done, or are currently doing some form of re-engineering. Clearly, redesigning the organisation's processes is not a new idea, indeed it is an essential part of the management function. What distinguishes BPR from just ordinary management is a philosophical one. It endorses a willingness to completely discard established and tested ideas in favour of innovative untried ones. BPR is about asking fundamental questions, and attacking assumptions that drive the conduct of the business. Michael Hammer, one of the champions of BPR, argues that organisations are riddled with outdated and obsolete rules and procedures often based on incorrect assumptions. The job of re-engineering is to challenge the status quo by asking the following questions:

1.   Why do we do what we do?

2.   Why do we do it the way we do?

There are a number of key features which distinguish a BPR programme from other popular initiatives. BPR includes both radical and dramatic change, and involves process redesign. It is radical in that it seeks to address root causes, often opting for abandoning what is currently in place, starting from the beginning, and inventing completely new ways of work. Therefore the focus is on invention, rather than improvement, modification, or enhancement. BPR is dramatic in that it is not about fine tuning and making marginal improvements, but rather about achieving leaps in performance. BPR is about processes. A process is a collection of activities or tasks that are liked together in a coordinated manner to achieve a specific objective. BPR tries to redefine activities and redesign how they link together to form a process. However, BPR is commonly misunderstood to deal with only technical issues, particularly computer automation. BPR equally considers the social aspects of process redesign such as organisational behaviour, staffing issues, policies, incentives, and employee satisfaction and growth. Hence technology and people are the critical factors in re-engineering the business process.

It is easier to define BPR than to describe how it is done. This is because it is a creative process, and depends on the unique context of the company and its environment. Michael Hammer provides a detailed description of how BPR is accomplished by using a number of cases as illustration. Through his analysis, five stages of BPR implementation are identified:

1. **Preparing the Organisation.** In order to conduct a BPR programme, the people in the organisation must be prepared to spend a considerable amount of time and energy, and therefore must be organised and motivated in advance. In addition, a general plan of action must be prepared, deciding where, what, and how to focus the initiative.

2. **Identifying Process Components.** An understanding of the internal and external processes must be developed. This requires the naming of activities, and linking them together using process maps to identify processes. It is also important to attach descriptive labels to activities, such as identifying them as value-added, discretionary, support, or primary.

3. **Forming the Vision.** After identifying 'what is', a vision is needed to create a foundation for 'what should be'. The new vision should be capable of achieving breakthrough performance. The vision should first be expressed in broad terms with general statements about what things should look like after re-engineering. This should then be refined in more detailed objectives like reduce physical storage and automate voucher work-flow.

4. **Developing Technical and Social Solutions.** Specific actions, procedures, rules, and policies must be developed to achieve the vision of 'what should be'. Often activity maps are used to formulate proposed process redesign schemes. In addition, staffing, recruitment, and education and training solutions are needed to support technical changes.

5. **Transformation.** Technical and social solutions must be executed to realise the new process vision. Often pilot projects are used to test solutions before they are instituted company-wide.

In today's world of intense competition, good financial controls and attention to financial indicators no longer ensure survival. There must be a search for continual improvement. Focusing on process redesign is an essential survival tool for modern businesses. However, BPR is not easy to do. Experience shows that such radical redesign normally takes between three and five years to complete. Such companies as Eastman Kodak, AT&T, and Caterpillar have gone through BPR, and attest to its difficulties as well as its benefits.

Functional Cost Analysis

Functional cost analysis is a cost management technique that focuses on the various functions and design features of a product. It is used to reduce product costs while maintaining or even improving customer satisfaction. It is most often applied to physical products, but can also be used for services.

Functional analysis is of greatest use in the design stage of a product's life cycle, because this is where functional attributes are conceived. The aim is to satisfy customers by ensuring that products incorporate specific functions desired by the customer. However, customers are only willing to pay a certain amount for a specific function, and therefore, both cost and the level of importance the customer attaches to a specific function are part of the analysis. For example, most automobile owners would agree that electric car windows are a desired function. However, this does not mean that all customer are willing to pay the added costs for this function and this is why automobile manufacturers continue to make cars with manual widows.

Functional cost analysis is performed by comparing the cost of each function of a product with the perceived benefit obtained by the customer. If the cost of the function exceeds the benefit to the customer, then the function should be either eliminated, modified to reduce its costs, or enhanced in terms of its perceived value.

Functional cost analysis is based on the construction of a functional tree. This is a diagram consisting of each function of the product, relating functions, purposes, and physical parts. It is constructed by first identifying the main purpose of the product and then breaking it down into sub-purposes. Each sub-purpose is then matched up with the actual parts on the product. To illustrate, consider a furniture manufacturer building a functional tree for a simple wooden chair. Management begins by asking what is the main purpose and sub-purposes of the chair, and which parts serve these purposes? A functional tree for a chair might look like that presented in Figure 6.5.

Even a very simple product like a chair can be broken down into many different functions and components. Building a functional tree allows management to connect the physical nature of the product with the perceived benefit to the customer. The analysis goes further by examining each part of the product and identifying its unique role. Here, management is asking 'why does the part exist?' Figure 6.6 illustrates how the parts of a chair might be linked to specific functions of the product.

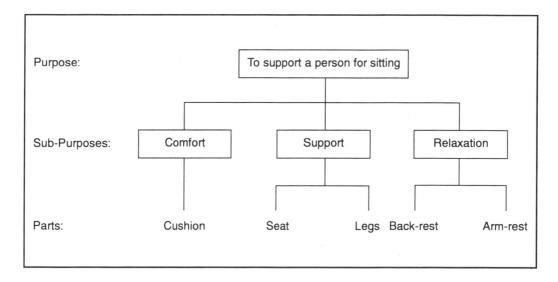

Figure 6.5 Functional tree of a chair.

Part name	Function
Legs	To raise level of sitting position
Back-rest	To support the back of a sitting person
Arm-rest	To support the arms of a sitting person
Horizontal plane	To support the buttocks of a sitting person
Cushion	To add comfort to a sitting person

Figure 6.6 Functional role of chair parts.

In order to complete the functional analysis, management must collect two additional variables:

1.   The approximate cost of each part

2.   The perceived value of each part/function

The cost for each part can be determined using direct costs alone such as direct materials and labour but may also include some allocated portion of overhead. However, to collect perceptions of customers, management must go outside the firm. To do this, companies normally conduct surveys and interviews to determine which functions of the product give the most value to customers. In our chair example, we might use a ranking system from 1 to 10 to gauge the importance of the function to the customer, with 10 representing the highest value. The cost and relative ranking of importance of each function can then be compared by calculating a cost-benefit score as presented in Figure 6.7 below.

Part name	Unit cost	Importance rank	Benefit score/cost
A. Legs	£12.00	6 points	.50
B. Back-rest	£ 3.00	7 points	2.33
C. Arm-rest	£ 6.00	2 points	.33
D. Horizontal plane	£17.00	10 points	.59
E. Cushion	£14.00	3 points	.21

Figure 6.7 Functional role of chair parts.

Although the cost/benefit score means little in isolation, it does provide a useful measure for evaluating the relative contribution each function adds to the value of the product. For example, we can see from this analysis that the customers consider the seat the most important function of the chair while the least important is the cushion. However, management should recognise that the importance rank will vary among different customer groups. For example, while the cushion part of the seat might rank low in importance for temporary seating situations (e.g. photo-booth), customers requiring extended seating conditions (e.g. transatlantic airline passengers) might rank the cushion higher up on the scale. Therefore, management must be very specific in terms of the target customers intended to be served by the functions of the product.

We can also see from the analysis in Figure 6.7 that the most costly part of the chair is the seat and the least costly is the back-rest. Management must analyse the relationship between cost and price, which is done by constructing an analysis grid, plotting each part of the product along a two dimensional axis (cost and importance-rank) like that presented in Figure 6.8 below.

The top left quadrant represents the part with the highest cost and least perceived benefit. Parts in this quadrant might be targeted for dropping or redesign. In this case, the cushion is very expensive relative to the other parts and is not valued very highly by the customer. Perhaps the chair is manufactured for use in an elementary school where cushions tend to get abused and are not really needed. One method of rectifying this problem is to eliminate the cushion thus making the product more price competitive, or perhaps anther option would be to reduce the cost of materials used in the cushion thus increasing its cost/benefit score.

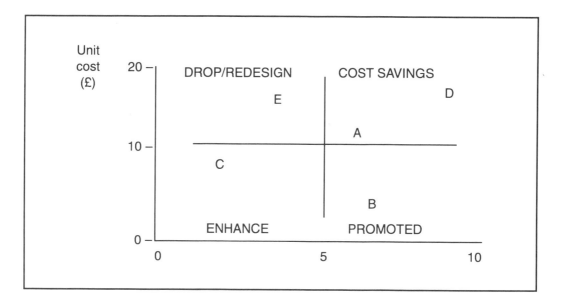

Figure 6.8 Functional analysis grid.

The bottom right quadrant is just the opposite. It represents the best possible or ideal position for a function or part. It is where the cost of the part is the lowest and the perceived benefit to the customer is the highest relative to other functions. These functions should be advertised and promoted as the most sellable aspect of the product. According to the analysis, the back-rest is relatively cheap to produce while it provides the customer with a significant amount of benefit.

The top right quadrant represents the highest costs as well as the highest perceived benefit to the customer. These parts are considered essential to the product and cannot be eliminated without degrading the product. However, parts in this quadrant do provide an opportunity for cost reduction.

The bottom left quadrant represents the lowest costs and lowest value parts. Because the costs are already low, there is little opportunity for further cost reduction. However, management might focus on enhancing the function to increase the perceived benefit to the customer.

Implementing functional analysis in an organisation consists of eight basic steps:

Step 1: Choose object of analysis. The object of analysis could be just about anything that management wants to investigate. Normally, these are products, services, or overhead areas of the company. It is suggested first select a product or service that has the highest potential for improvement which is likely to be one that is high in volume and complex to produce.

Step 2: Form implementation team. It is important to look at the product from a broad perspective. Therefore, the team should be composed of managers from many different areas of the company. Normally, accounting, marketing, production, and purchasing departments are essential to gain a full appreciation of the functional dimensions of a product.

Step 3: Collect data. Information must be collected both internally and externally. Internal information includes product functions and specifications, parts, assemblies, design details, manufacturing processes, target markets, and cost profiles. External information includes customer responses to questions about the product reliability, quality, uses, benefits, and the relative importance attached to different functions. Normally, questionnaires or interviews are formulated so that the results can be easily managed and incorporated into the analysis. For example, the importance a customer gives to a function might be classified as high, medium or low, rather than a descriptive statement.

Step 4: Construct functional tree diagram. As described earlier, a functional tree is a technique for arranging the different functions of a product in a logical order to facilitate analysis.

Step 5: Evaluate functions. At this step all the data is brought together, focusing on the functions of the product. Here, the cost and benefits of each function are compared by calculating a cost/benefit score as described above. Then it is useful to plot each function on a two dimensional grid to help give insight into the available options.

Step 6: Implement selected option. Based on the functional analysis, management must execute one or more of the options available. This may include eliminating or promoting a specific function. It may also include modifying or enhancing functions.

Step 7: Review results. The final step is to assess the consequences of implementing the option, and what additional measures are needed to continue or adapt to changes in the organisation and the market place.

Functional analysis adds a strategic dimension to managerial accounting. It links internal costing information with the external demands of the market place. Using functional analysis, management accountants can provide information that can help design or redesign products, assist in targeting marketing efforts, and provide a basis for cost control that is sensitive to market considerations.

7 Supporting decision making

Introduction

This chapter outlines some of the important ways in which the management accountant can provide decision support for management. Primarily this comes in the form of information on the financial implications of decisions and the alternative courses of action which the decision maker faces. In a world of uncertainty qualitative factors and the ability to quickly assess 'what if' questions and the sentitivity of decisions to key variables have also become a necessary part of the management accounting function. Thus definitive financial projections should be informed by strategy and also treated with some caution.

Capital Investment Decisions

Capital investment decisions are central to the fabric and the success of organisations. Fortunately there are several well established financial techniques available to support management in making key decisions on the acquisition of the assets which will underlie the future survival and earning potential of the business. These include the payback period and discounting techniques based on the time value of money. Of the latter the internal rate of return and net present value are most prominent.

However the results of these techniques are only as good as the quality of the information to which they are applied. As they require estimates of future changes in cash flows stemming from the initial investment the accuracy and reliability of their results is heavily dependent on the complexity of the situations to which they are applied. Decisions involving major changes in technology (investments in flexible manufacturing and computer aided manufacturing systems) and often related new work process methods (scheduling systems such as just-in-time) have proved extremely difficult to model adequately in financial terms. Consequently the adequacy of the conventional approaches to the capital investment decision in such cases have been subject to considerable criticism.

Capital Investments in Complex Technology

A number of modifications to the conventional approaches to investment analysis have been suggested as means of overcoming the complexity of sophisticated technological investment.

1. Accept the fact that many of the potential cash inflow estimates will be extremely tentative. Split the benefits into those which are tangible and those which are intangible. The tangible benefits which can more readily be estimated in cash flow terms include stock reductions, space savings, employee reductions and quality improvements (in terms of waste and returns reductions). The more intangible benefits include the flexibility of response to customer demands, the offer of enhanced speed of service, the knowledge gained on how to integrate a technological development and how to cope with change. Conventional discounting can be applied to the investment costs and tangible benefits. An estimate can then be made of the amount of intangible benefits needed to make the investment financially viable. This figure can be assessed against the qualitative description of intangible benefits.

2. Consider the strategic implications of investment decisions. Complex technological investments are a key part of an organisation's competitive strategy. The cash flow implications are therefore dynamic in the sense that they not only have an internal effect but also an impact on competitors. The latter effects will depend on the competitor's reactions which may be difficult to second guess. However the cash flow consequences of these types of investment should not be determined by comparison with the status quo in pricing market share or cost structure. All of these characteristics are likely to change without the investment as rivals' positions in the market may be strengthened. Cash flows are dependent not only on our own actions but also the actions of others. To some extent competitive dynamics can be taken into account by considering the source of future cash benefits. If these are won from existing competitors' revenues they may be worth more (and perhaps therefore should be weighted more heavily in DCF calculations) in the longer run than those achieved from say an internal cost saving. In the end beating the competition is a major objective of investment and should be reflected in the appraisal of opportunities. At a strategic level consideration should also be given to the effects of investment decisions across the value chain. Does a new technology allow supply to be provided more cheaply or flexibly? Does it impact on the efficiency and cost of our customers when using our supplies? How does it influence the key cost drivers in our direct activities and support services?

Does it enhance reputation, product quality and other goodwill attributes? Attention should be given to these types of question even if that attention does not result in hard cash flow forecasts.

3.   The integration of conventional cash flow analysis and more complex dimensions of the investment decision requires a structured checklist. Figure 7.1 contains a matrix of the strategic implications of investment decisions and the potential benefits which may be derived therefrom. This framework allows some conventional quantification but also highlights the many cells where this is difficult and qualitative assessment is more likely. Consideration of each cell is invited by the decision structure and this helps to ensure a more comprehensive appraisal than would be achieved by traditional approaches alone.

Strategies/ benefits															
Product enhancement	X*					X**									
New products	X*			X*			X**	X**							
Risk reduction				X**											
Cost advantages		X*		X											
Improved organisation structure															
Companywide impact															
Monetary items															
Items which can be expressed in monetary terms*															
Scored items**															
TOTALS															

* items which can be converted into monetary terms.
** items which can be expressed in monetary terms scored on a single 'points' scale (1 to 10).

Figure 7.1 Strategic planning matrix.

Source: M. Bromwich and A. Bhimani, 'Strategic Investment Appraisal', Management Accounting, March 1991, p.48.

ABC and Developments in Contribution Margin Analysis

The contribution margin (sales value less variable cost) provides a basis for making short-term decisions on product mix, use of spare resources and pricing. Moreover it provides a basis for break-even analysis and basic business modelling. However it is based on the simplistic notion that costs either vary proportionately with production output or are fixed. With the development of Activity-Based Costing (ABC) concepts, the traditional contribution margin can be adapted to generate more sophisticated and useful decision making information. ABC can enhance the application of the contribution margin approach by first expanding the notion of cost variability, and second by incorporating relevant qualitative variables.

The traditional contribution margin approach only considers cost variation based on unit volume. This is a dangerous assumption because often management interprets unchanging costs as unmanageable costs. ABC highlights the potential distortions which may occur when using a single unit-level variation base.

With ABC it is assumed that cost behaviour is much more complex and fluctuates in response to factors other than production volume. Product complexity, variety, flexibility, quality and service are all dimensions of activity which change and which can influence costs significantly. As discussed in Chapter 5, cost drivers can be used to predict and measure how resources are consumed by the various dimensions of work performance. Cost drivers may include a variety of work measures including, for example, number of purchase orders, machine hours, number of set-ups, or number of customer orders. They can also be categorised into four different types of cost variation: unit-level, batch-level, product-level, and facility-level. This hierarchy of cost variation is designed to capture the real world complexity of cost behaviour, and can be used to improve the predictive value of the contribution margin approach.

ABC assumes that resources are consumed by activities and the manner in which activities consume costs determines the basis of cost variability. Unit level activity costs are those which would approximately change with the volume of units produced. An activity such as drilling holes on each part would be considered a unit-level activity cost because it is likely to vary proportionately with production volume. Batch-level variation occurs with such activities as setting up machines or ordering a group of parts for a batched production run. These costs are relatively independent of the number of units produced, but increment with respect to the number of batches. Product-sustaining activity costs are performed to support different product lines. Maintaining product specifications, performing engineering changes, and expediting products are all examples of product sustaining activity costs. These costs are variable with changes to product lines, but they are relatively fixed in relation to production volume or number of batches. Product level costs can be incurred even if no unit production occurs at all.

Unit, batch, and production-sustaining activity costs may be reasonably assigned to individual products. However, facility-sustaining costs enable all production to occur, but tend to be independent of product volume and mix in the short-term. General insurance, accounting services, and general administration are examples of facility-sustaining costs. These costs could be classified as fixed with respect to all of the other variation bases. Cost variation of facility based costs will occur with respect to changes in the facility of the organisation. With ABC, all costs are considered to have potential variation within their respective cost hierarchies. Costs within one hierarchical level are likely to be fixed with respect to another level. It is assumed, however, that all costs within a specific hierarchical level will vary approximately in proportion to the quality of that level's activity cost driver.

An ABC system identifies all the activities performed to produce and deliver a firm's output. However, the identification of activities does not, of itself, necessarily indicate their relevance in a decision model. Many firms incorporate a coding scheme to add qualitative, decision useful features to the model. These schemes can vary from simple dichotomous ones, such as value-added or non-value-added, necessary or unnecessary, or to complex schemes such as reason codes which provide insight into why activities are performed, purpose codes which provide insight into whether the purpose of the activity is central or peripheral to the mission of the firm, and control codes which identify the extent to which activities are controllable. Attribute coding is thus a vehicle by which qualitative information is incorporated into the contribution model. It permits management to enhance traditional cost information to allow for a more complex representation of economic reality.

In the past, qualitative variables have been difficult to incorporate into a model that depends greatly on quantifiable variables. In order to fit such variables efficiently into a decision model, they must be assigned a manageable scope and identifiable unit of measurement. A manageable scope defines the range of control which management can exercise over costs. The unit of measurement is the establishment of incremental variables or cost drivers by which to measure complex cost behaviour patterns. The contribution margin approach depends on the establishment of quantifiable relationships to break down problems in a useful manner and aid in cost predictability. Understanding that usefulness, rather than complete accuracy, should be the focus through a systematic categorisation of selected descriptive attributes is necessary. For example, the attribute of controllability may simply be defined in terms of high, medium and low. The scope of controllability can be measured by devising a satisfactory 'rule of thumb' to aid in the hierarchy designation. For example, a high controllable cost may be assessed in terms of management's expectation of its ability to reasonably eliminate 90% of the cost within one year. A low controllable cost may be based on management's expectation that only 10% of the costs can reasonably be eliminated within one year.

Rather than forcing all variable costs into a single incremental section of the model, multiple sections can be added reflecting control layers. Those costs which are ranked as highly controllable can be more confidently expected to realise short-run cost savings. Those costs ranked as low in controllability terms provide less confidence that these costs will be relevant in the short term.

An illustration of a multi-activity based contribution margin approach using the controllability attribute is presented below in Figure 7.2.

Activity-name	total cost	control	basis of cost variability	base-#
purchase order processing	£20,000	high	batch	300
setting up	5,000	high	batch	300
facility maintenance	10,000	low	facility	1
expediting	7,000	medium	batch	300
engineering changes	3,000	high	product	1
production testing	12,000	medium	unit	2000
inspecting	3,000	high	unit	2000
Direct costs:				
direct material cost	60,000	high	unit	2000
direct labour cost	90,000	low	unit	2000
Total costs	£210,000			

Figure 7.2 Activity information.

The first column represents the amount of cost traced to the activity using ABC. The second column is the ranking of the qualitative attribute of controllability. The third column is the designated cost variation base. The last column is the number of occurrences of the cost variation base. For example, there were 2,000 units, 300 batches, and 1 product and 1 facility occurrences.

To accommodate the new features of multiple cost variation bases and the attribute of controllability, the model must take on a two dimensional format. The horizontal axis represents cost variation bases and the vertical axis represents cost control aspects. A multi-level two-dimensional cost model can now be constructed. This is presented in Figure 7.3 below.

Level of Controllability	Basis of Variability			
	unit	batch	product	facility
HIGH: controllable activity costs:				
direct materials	£30.0			
purchase order processing		£66.7		
setting up		16.7		
engineering changes			£3,000.0	
inspecting	1.5			
HIGH controllable costs total	31.5	83.4	3,000.0	£0.0
MED: controllable activity costs:				
expediting		23.3		
production testing	6.0			
MED controllable costs total	6.0	23.3	0.0	0.0
LOW: controllable activity costs:				
facility maintenance				10,000.0
direct labour	45.0			
LOW controllable costs total	45.0	0.0	0.0	10,000.0
TOTAL controllable costs	£82.5	£106.7	£3,000.0	£10,000.0

Figure 7.3 ABC cost composition model.

There are two important distinctions to make about the ABC cost composition model. First, activities rather than cost elements are used to represent cost. Second, there is no single cost calculated to represent incremental costs. All activities that conform to a unit-based cost variation are aligned in the unit column. All activities that conform to a batch-base variation are listed under that heading. At the same time the corresponding control level is designated. Those costs which appear closest to the top of the model are more likely to behave in the manner described by the variation base under which it is listed because they are more controllable. On the other hand, those costs near the bottom of the model are constrained in some manner and are less likely to behave according to the hierarchical variation base. In other words, costs that are classified as highly controllable are more likely to behave as expected. A conservative approach to this analysis might be to limit predictions to the upper part of the model.

Constructing a multi-layered contribution margin analysis statement incorporating qualitative attributes requires a three step process:

1.   **Gather ABC information.** Collect the activity costs, relevant qualitative attributes, and cost variation base transactions.

2.   **Construct the cost model.** Order activity information in a two dimensional model depicting a single attribute (eg. controllability) along the vertical axis and cost variation bases (unit, batch, product, facility) along the horizontal axis.

3.   **Apply model to decision making.** Use model for predicting cost behaviour, and making operational and strategic decisions.

Contribution margin analysis is an important tool which can be applied to help managers organise, summarise, and simplify complex cost data. It is a systematic and efficient method of evaluating cost information and predicting outcomes in response to short-term production decisions. Over the years it has undergone little modification. With the introduction of ABC systems and computer technology, the contribution model has the opportunity of evolving into a more reliable and flexible tool for decision making. Qualitative factors such as managerial control can be incorporated into the model using coding schemes and multiple variation bases can be incorporated using activity analysis, and these provide management with the capacity to more accurately predict cost behaviour.

The Potential Cost for Modelling within an ABC Framework

Models are summarisations and simplifications of a more complex and dynamic world. All that managers can reasonably expect from a model is an organised and systematic approach to managing information in order to help approximate probable outcomes of decisions.

Models can be decision specific, a new one tailored to each situation. While this approach may be appropriate for large scale projects requiring long-term investment and capital considerations, it is inappropriate and indeed impractical for 'everyday' short-term decisions which require speed and low cost implementation. Managers must always balance the cost of accuracy with the benefits expected from the information. While a systematic approach is not always appropriate to decision problems, it can be faster, more efficient, and less expensive than an in-depth study. Moreover, outcomes from an in-depth study may not be materially different from a systematic decision model.

An ABC system is a model depicting a view of the organisation based upon the work undertaken within it. However, it has a limited applicability to decision making. ABC systems have proven useful for making operational changes based on resource usage, but have failed to inform management about spending (i.e. cash flow) changes. This is because ABC was designed to measure the rate of resource demand (activity) as opposed to the rate of resource supply (spending). One of the most important criteria for a good model is its ability to translate proposed courses of action into incremental cash flow projections. Therefore, in order for ABC to fully accommodate managerial decision making needs, modelling is needed to translate changes in resource demand (activity information) into changes in resource supply (cash flow).

Until recently, it was implicit in ABC methodology that changes in resource demand would result in proportional changes in resource supply (spending). It was assumed that expected supply (future spending) would be changed by the relative proportion of current supply (s_0) to current demand (d_0). For example a reduction in purchasing activity of 105 (as measured by cost driver volume) would result in 10% less spending or purchasing. This is expressed as follows:

$$s_1 = d_1 \, (s_0 / \, d_0)$$

Where expected demand is d_1 and expected supply is s_1, and current demand and supply as d_0 and s_1 respectively.

For example, consider the activity of processing purchase orders. Assume that the current amount of total resources (expenses) traced to this activity is £5,000 (s_0) and the current number of purchase orders is 100 (d_0). If the number of purchase orders processed (resource demand) increases from 100 to 200, then management would expect spending to double. This is computed as follows:

$$£10,000 = 200 \, (£5,000 \, / \, 100)$$

After many attempts at applying ABC in this way, it was revealed that changes in cost driver demand greatly overstated the impact on spending. This is a result of confusion between resource supply and demand. When managers assess how much costs would change with respect to a particular decision (e.g. add or drop, change a process, or impose minimum order sizes), they are interested in spending changes in the short term and ABC is not intended to provide this information. Rather, ABC systems measure the cost of using resources, not the cost of supplying them. The difference between resources supplied and resources consumed or demanded through activities represents unused capacity for the period. This is expressed in the following logic-statements:

Unused capacity = s_0 - [(d_0 (s_0 / dc_0)] and

Used capacity = d_0 (s_0 / dc_0) and consequently

Current resource supply = used capacity + unused capacity.

Expressed as:

s_0 = d_0 (s_0 / dc_0) + s_0 - [(d_0 (s_0 / dc_0)] therefore, as long as

Current capacity (dc_0) _ expected demand (d_1)

Expected supply = expected demand + expected unused capacity.

Expressed as:

s_1 = d_1 (s_0 / dc_0) + (dc_0 - d_1) (s_0 / dc_0)

For example, recall that the total current resources supply to the activity of processing purchase orders is £5,000 (s_0). If the current capacity for the activity of processing purchase orders is 400 purchase orders (dc_0) and the current demand is only 100 (d_0), then there is excess capacity of 300 (400 - 100) purchase orders. Therefore, increases in demand should not increase resource supply requirements until excess capacity has been reduced to zero. In this case, since excess capacity is greater than zero (300) then expected resource supply (s_1) is equal to current resource supply (s_0). This is expressed using the above equation as follows:

s_1 = 100 (£5,000 / 400) + £5,000 - [(100 (£5,000 / 400)] =

s_1 = £1,250 + £3,750, and therefore, s_1 = £5,000

According to this example, £1,250 represents the cost of resources used and £3,750 represents the cost of unused capacity. Therefore, only 25% (£1,250/£5,000) of the resource is consumed by the activity. As long as excess capacity exists, no increase in resource supply is expected. To illustrate this point further, assume that the number of purchase orders increases dramatically from 100 to 350. Using the equation above, the expected resource supply (s_1) is computed as follows:

$s_1 = 350 \ (£5{,}000 \ / \ 400) + (400 - 350) \ (£5{,}000 \ / \ 400)$

$s_1 = £4{,}375 + £625 = s_1 = £5{,}000$, and therefore

Expected supply (s_1) remains equal to current supply (s_0)

Even as resource demand increases from 100 to 350 purchase orders, the level of resource supply remains the same at £5,000. In this example, there has been an increase in the level of resources consumed by the activity, which has resulted in a reduction in the cost of unused capacity from £3,750 to £625, but no change in spending has occurred.

Because activity costs represent resource demand, additional variables are needed if activity based systems are to be used for modelling spending changes. The first new variable needed is called the ISI (Incremental Supply Interval), which represents the estimated incremental change in spending (expressed in monetary units) necessary to accommodate the expected level of capacity from d_0 to d_1. The second variable is called the Incremental Demand Interval (IDI), which represents the incremental change in capacity (expressed in cost driver units) made available from a change in spending. A new layer of capacity could be expressed both in monetary terms and in cost driver terms. The ISI represents the incremental monetary investment necessary to increase capacity to accommodate projected increases in demand from activities beyond the current level of capacity. It could also represent the opportunity for incremental cost savings in response to decreases in demand below capacity. The IDI could be thought of as the ISI expressed in cost driver units.

The ISI is formulated by analysing the market acquisition characteristics of a particular resource which determine the flexibility of its supply. For example, consider the prospects of adding new personnel resources (salary expense) to the activity of processing purchase orders. The market place for acquiring human resources does not normally permit people to be hired in excessively small increments. Therefore, the ISI for this resource/activity relationship could be the cost of hiring a part-time or temporary purchase order clerk. Since the market place does not permit hiring workers to process only a few purchase orders it is likely that excess capacity will have to be acquired. For example, assume the current supply of resources is one clerk at £10,000 per year who has a capacity of processing 100 purchase orders. Further assume that management expects the internal demand of this activity to increase from 100 to 115 purchase orders. Since the market characteristics for acquiring human resources does not permit employing a worker to process only 15 purchase orders a year, management would have to invest in excess capacity by employing a part-time worker who may have the capacity to process 50 purchase orders (the IDI) for a cost of £5,000 (the ISI) a year. In this case, management is forced to purchase excess capacity of 35 purchase order (50 - 15).

In order to model changes in resource demand, the ISI and the IDI variables must be integrated in the equation which must express the changes in supply and demand in relation to the level of capacity. Expected supply (s1) could be predicted by modelling the changes in demand using the following step function equation:

$$s_1 = ISI \{ d_1 / IDI \} + ISI$$

where the brackets { } denote an integer function (e.g. {3.1} = 3)

For example, consider again the activity of processing purchase orders. In the interest of simplicity, assume that only two resources have been traced to this activity: a highly pushed[1] resource, office rent in the amount of £10,000 per year; and a highly pulled[2] resource, telephone call charges in the amount of £6,000 per year. Further assume that these resources allow for a maximum current capacity of 400 (dc_0) purchase orders to be processed per year. Processing purchase orders beyond this point without additional resources would result in some form of organisational pain, such as delays and other forms of quality erosion, indicating to management that the practical capacity threshold has been exceeded. The question is, if management expects to be processing 600 purchase orders next year because of new business, how much new spending would be required to accommodate the increase in demand from this activity?

To analyse the impact on spending, each resource must be considered separately as it relates to the demand from the activity, thus forming a unique resource/activity relationship. Because telephone call charge is a highly pulled resource, excess capacity is likely to be zero (or close to zero) and thus would exhibit a different cost behaviour pattern than office rent. Therefore, expected spending with regard to telephone expense could be reasonably predicted using the linear equation; $s_1 = d_1 (s_0 / d_0)$ described earlier. This is computed as follows:

---

1   A pushed resource is one that is supplied in advance of demand, often resulting in excess capacity.

2   A pulled resource is one in which demand initiates supply, and is likely to result in no excess capacity. Pulled resources are supplied as needed, and management possesses considerable flexibility in controlling their use.

$$s_1 = 600 \ (£6,000 \ / \ 400) = s_1 = £9,000$$

The supply and demand relationship is expressed as a smooth upward slope and is presented in Figure 7.4 below.

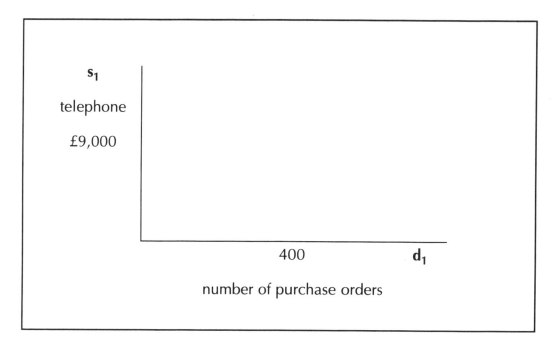

Figure 7.4 Relationship between telephone expense and POs.

For any value of d_1, a proportional change in s_1 occurs. For example in Figure 7.4, the slope is expressed as $s_1 = 15(d_1)$. Therefore, if d_1 is equal to 100 then s_1 is equal to 1,500, and if d_1 is equal to 101 then s_1 is equal to 1,515.

Spending changes for office rent will most likely result in excess capacity because physical facilities cannot be supplied in small increments. In order to add more floor space to accommodate increases in demand, management must invest in new facilities by either buying or renting office space. Assume that management estimates that a future incremental layer of capacity would require an investment of £8,000 (the ISI) which would permit an estimated increment of 350 (the IDI) additional purchase orders to be processed. By using the step function $s_1 = ISI \ \{ \ d_1 \ / \ IDI\} + ISI$, a model of the supply and demand could be constructed. Any value for estimated demand could be plugged into the equation to get a value for supply along the step function slope. This is the resource/activity relationship presented in Figure 7.5 below.

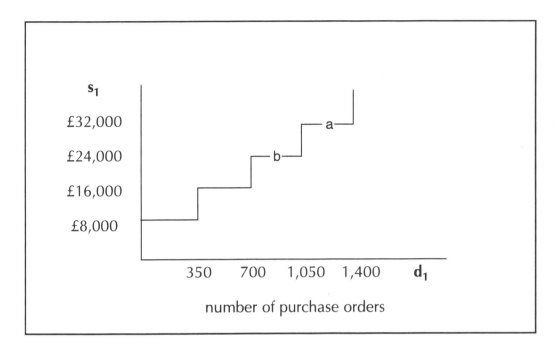

Figure 7.4 Relationship between rent and POs.

The level of spending will depend on whether the current layer of capacity is greater than or equal to zero. If no excess capacity exists, a change in demand will result in a change in supply by the value of the ISI. In contrast, if excess capacity is greater than zero then s_1 will be equal to s_0 and no new spending is required. For example, looking back at Figure 7.5, when d_1 is equal to zero then s_1 is equal to £8,000, and when d1 increases to 349 then s1 is still equal to £8,000. However, once demand reaches 350 (dc_0), then excess capacity has been reduced to zero ($d_1 = dc_0$), and spending jumps up to £16,000 creating a new capacity layer.

The vertical jumps in the slope steps represent the ISI and the horizontal movements represent the IDI. The step function in Figure 7.5 indicates that changes in demand will not have an impact on supply until current capacity reaches zero. Once capacity is reached, the change in supply would be equal to the value of the ISI. Highly pulled resources in which supply is very flexible with demand would have very small vertical jumps in the line, indicating a small ISI value. In fact, a purely pulled resource would be depicted as a smooth upward sloping line without steps, and with an ISI equal to zero. In contrast, highly pushed resources would exhibit larger vertical jumps in the slope, depicting the inflexibility of supply to changes in demand from activities.

Using the model in Figure 7.5, spending requirements can be estimated for both increases and decreases in projected demand. For example, if the number of purchase orders grew significantly to 1,300 (at point 'a' in Figure

7.5), the level of spending required to accommodate this demand would be estimated at £32,000. This is computed as follows:

$$s_1 = £8,000 \{ 1,300 / 350 \} + £8,000 = s_1 = £32,000$$

On the other hand, if management discovered a way to reduce the number of purchase orders through process redesign efforts to 800 (at point 'b' in Figure 7.5), the necessary supply level would be reduced to £24,000, resulting in the opportunity for savings of £8,000 (£32,000 - £24,000). This is computed as follows:

$$s_1 = £8,000 \{ 800 / 350 \} + £8,000 = s_1 = £24,000$$

where potential savings are equal to: $s_0 - s_1$

Note that changes in demand for pushed resources are not proportional to changes in supply. Rather, changes in spending depend upon the degree of supply flexibility. Market characteristics determine the extent of flexibility, and therefore the size of the ISI and the IDI. Using these variables in a step function equation provides a model for predicting the economic consequences of proposed operational decisions which involve changes in demand from activities.

So far the model has assumed a one-to-one relationship between a resource and an activity. Clearly, the organisational environment is more complex, involving many interrelated connections between resource supply and demand. Organisational resources are consumed by many activities in the company and, consequently, an activity cost may be composed of a combination of varying degrees of pushed and pulled resources. In addition, each activity is likely to have a different cost driver representing the consumption of resources assigned to it. The model essentially attempts to express the change from d_0 to d_1 by quantifying the change from s_0 to s_1, using the ISI and the IDI inside a step function equation. However, since there is likely to be more than one resource traced to a specific activity, the economic consequences are likely to involve many different spending/activity relationships. Therefore, the total spending change which results from operational changes in demand is composed of the changes in s_1 for every resource affected by the change. This is expressed as follows:

Total spending = s_1 of resource A + s_1 of resource B + s_1 of resource C... or

Total spending = Σs_1

Therefore total change in spending could be expressed as:

$$\Delta s = (\Sigma s_1 - \Sigma s_0)$$

In order to use the step function described above to predict spending behaviour, proposed operational decisions must be translated into cost driver terms. Thus, the cost drivers serve as the linking mechanism for reconciling resource supply and demand. Applying this concept in practice requires a three step process.

1. **Determine cost driver impact.** The decision or proposed action must be translated into a set of estimated cost driver changes. For example, if management is considering a new product line, an estimation of how many new purchase orders, machine set-ups, invoices, batches, and sales calls is needed. Similarly, if management discovers a way to improve the production process, an estimation of how many labour and machine hours, set-ups and stock movements can be saved is needed.

2. **Determine relevant activities.** Relevant activities are those which are driven by cost drivers which are expected to change as a result of the proposed action. For example, if the proposed action requires more purchase orders to be processed then the activity of processing purchase orders becomes a relevant activity. Similarly, if an increase in the number of sales calls is expected, the activity of making sales calls becomes relevant to the decision.

3. **Establish a step function relationship between relevant activities and resources.** A step function equation using ISI and IDI variables must be established for each resource that is traced to each relevant activity. However, when a single resource is traced to more than one activity, the relationship with the largest ISI must be used to estimate the change in spending. For example, if both the activity of making sales calls and the activity of processing purchase orders require an increase (according to the ISI) in the demand for telephone service, then the new capacity must be the activity relationship which places the highest demand upon the resource. The process is summarised in Figure 7.6 below.

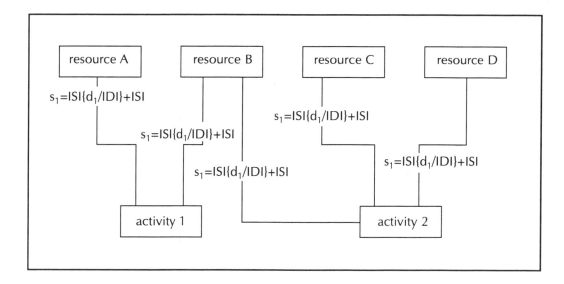

Figure 7.6 Multiple resource/activity relationships.

A step function exists for each activity/resource relationship. When a single resource (resource B) is consumed by more than one activity, more than one relationship exists and therefore more than one step function is needed to express it. However, since the new capacity of resource B is being determined from changes in demand from activities 1 and 2, only one relationship must be selected to predict spending changes. The relationship which requires the largest new spending is therefore the new capacity needed to satisfy the new demand.

As with any model, the step function approach described in this section is an oversimplification of reality. It reduces the complex and dynamic organisational environment to a system of predictable outcomes supported by a set of assumptions. There are a number of assumptions used in the model which could be questioned. For example, the ISI is assumed to be constant for each layer of demand. However, the market characteristics for acquiring resources are likely to fluctuate over time. For instance, the cost of office rent may increase over time as property values rise in response to economic conditions. In addition, the degree of supply flexibility may change as management perfects its control over spending, transforming pushed resources into pulled resources. An example of this has occurred over the last decade as businesses began to make extensive use of temporary workers. This has increased management's ability to adjust resource supply with demand. In spite of these assumptions and simplifications, the model is more realistic than the traditional approach based on fixed and variable costs and can therefore be a useful tool for decision making, as long as its limitations are considered.

8 Conclusion

The content of the previous seven chapters of this book provide ample evidence of the development and innovation which has occurred in management accounting in recent years. These changes have covered all of the key aspects of the management accounting function and provide scope for enhancing the role of the management accountant's contribution to setting strategy, guiding the organisation, taking stock of progress, improving performance and enhancing decision-making.

The reviews provided of each technique do not contain complete guidelines for implementation. The provision of a practical manual is outwith the scope of a publication of this size. Rather the text provides a checklist of ideas, hopefully several new, which the reader can appraise in terms of outline, and key benefits and limitations. It is thus a potential source of new practices which are worth considering as a basis for enhancing the information service provided by the management accounting function. Thus, for the reader, this report may provide a first step in the process of changing and improving management accounting. To continue the process the initial idea and assessment have to be followed up. To this end the further reading (Appendix A) has been carefully selected to reflect seminal contributions on each topic.

Without dynamism and change management accounting and management accountants run the danger of losing their importance within the firm. Changing technologies, products, organisational structures and management practices all lie at the heart of survival and success in a competitive environment. However these are also changes which impact upon how cost information should be produced, how budgets should be prepared and how performance should be measured. Yesterday's management accounting can therefore quickly become outmoded and its outputs irrelevant to those who use it. Management who create the demand for management accounting may lack the technical expertise to promote change. The onus therefore largely falls on the supply side (the management accountant) to initiate innovation and change. If the management accountants fail to do this their information supply role may be usurped by other information specialists within the firm.

Continuous improvement is a concept which can be applied to all spheres of business. The techniques illustrated in this book provide some ideas for the management accountant intent on encouraging this type of achievement in the accounting field. In the variety of management accounting practices now available lies the opportunity to design, for the modern business, a modern management accounting system.

Appendix A   Further reading

CHAPTER 2   STATEGIC MANAGEMENT ACCOUNTING
Bromwich, M. and Bhimani, A., *Pathways to Progress*, Chartered Institute of Management Accountants, 1994.

VALUE CHAIN ANALYSIS
Shank, J. and Govindarajan, V., *Strategic Cost Management and the Value Chain*, Journal of Cost Management, Winter 1992.

CUSTOMER PROFITABILITY ANALYSIS
Bellis-Jones, R., *Customer Profitability Analysis*, Management Accounting, Febuary 1989.

Porter, M., *Competitive Strategy*, The Free Press, New York, 1980.

SHAREHOLDER VALUE ANALYSIS
Mills, R.W., *Strategic Financial Management and Shareholder Value Analysis*, Management Accounting, March 1990.

CHAPTER 3   PLANNING AND OPERATIONAL VARIANCES
Demski, J.S., *Variance Analysis Using Constrained Linear Model* in D. Solomans (editor) Studies in Cost Analysis, Sweet and Maxwell, 1968.

ZERO BASED BUDGETS
Stonich, P., *Zero Base Planning – A Management Tool*, Management Planning, August 1976.

ACTIVITY BASED BUDGETS
Brimson, J., Fraser, R., *The Key Factors of ABB*, Management Accounting, January 1991.

TARGET COSTING
Tani, T., et al, *Target Cost Management in Japanese Companies: Current State of the Art*, Management Accounting Research, Vol. 5, 1994.

CHAPTER 4 RETURN ON INVESTMENT
Dearden, J., *Problems in Decentralised Profit Responsibility*, Harvard Business Review, May/June 1960.

RESIDUAL INCOME
Solomons, D., *Divisional Performance: Measurement and Control*, Financial Executive Research Foundation, 1965.

CRITICAL SUCCESS FACTORS
Rockart, J.F., *Chief Executives Define their own Data Needs*, Harvard Business Review, March/April 1979.

BALANCED SCORECARD
Kaplan, R., and Norton, D., *The Balanced Scorecard: Measures that Drive Performance*, Harvard Business Review, January/February 1992.

CHAPTER 5 ACTIVITY BASED COSTING
Cooper, R., *The Rise of Activity Based Costing*, Parts 1–4, Journal of Cost Management, 1988/89.

Innes, J. and Mitchell, F., A Survey of Activity-Based Costing in the UK's Largest Companies, *Management Accounting Research*, Vol. 6, 1995, pp. 137–153.

COST OF QUALITY
Paseward, R., *The Evolution of Quality Control Costs in American Manufacturing*, Journal of Cost Management, Spring 1991.

LIFE CYCLE COSTING
Shields, M., and Young, M., *Managing Product Life Cycle Costs: An Organizational Model*, Journal of Cost Management, Fall 1991.

CHAPTER 6 BENCHMARKING
Tucker, F., Zwan, S., and Camp, R., *How to Measure Yourself Against the Best*, Harvard Business Review, January/February 1987.

THEORY OF CONSTRAINTS
Goldratt, E., and Cox, J., *The Goal*, Gower Press, 1993.

BUSINESS PROCESS RE-ENGINEERING
Hammer, M., and Champy, J., *Re-engineering the Corporation*, Nicholas Brealey Publishing, 1993.

FUNCTIONAL COST ANALYSIS
Yoshikawa, T., Innes, J., and Mitchell, F., *Cost Management Through Functional Analysis*, Journal of Cost Management, Spring, 1989.

CHAPTER 7 CAPITAL INVESTMENT DECISIONS
Kaplan, R., *Must CIM be Justified by Faith alone?*, Harvard Business Review, March/April 1986.

CONTRIBUTION MARGIN AND DECISIONS
Cooper, R., and Kaplan, R., *Activity Based Systems: Measuring the Costs of Resource Usage*, Accounting Horizons, September 1992.